PATHWAYS TO GOD

A Study Guide to the Teachings of

SATHYA SAI BABA

by Jonathan Roof

LEELA PRESS INC.
A Non-Profit Company
Faber, VA

First published in 1991 by
Leela Press Inc.
Rt. 1, Box 339C
Faber, Virginia 22938

First printing

Library of Congress Cataloging-in-Publication Data

Pathways to God: A Study Guide to the Teachings of Sathya Sai Baba

ISBN 0-9629835-0-0

Cover Design by: Emily Scher
Photographs © Beth Topolski

Typeset in 11 point Times Roman
Printed in the United States of America by McNaughton & Gunn, Inc.

Dedicated to

Bhagavan Sri Sathya Sai Baba

Kali Yuga Avatar

CONTENTS

ACKNOWLEDGMENTS vii
FOREWORD ix

PART ONE: THE JOURNEY BEGINS

I. STUDY CIRCLE: A Tool for Transformation 1
    1. How Spiritual Training Begins, 1
    2. Study Circle's Purpose, 2
    3. Knowledge and Self-Confidence, 3
    4. A Typical Study Circle Routine, 3
    5. Suggested "Rules", 4
    6. The Goal of Self-Discovery, 6

II. ORGANIZATION: A Structure for Growth 7
    1. Why a Sai Organization? 7
    2. Rules, Timely Suggestions, 8
    3. Duties and Responsibilities of Officers, 10
    4. A Call to Action, 11

III. THE AVATAR: Light from Above 15
    1. What is an Avatar? 15
    2. When Darkness Threatens, 15
    3. The Nature of the Avatar, 18
    4. How to Recognize the Divine Being, 19
    5. How to Benefit from the Incarnation, 20

IV. FAITH: The Source of Knowledge 25
    1. All People Have Some Faith, 25
    2. The Origin of Belief, 25
    3. The Necessity of Faith, 26
    4. Guard the Tender Shoots, 27
    5. The Road to Victory, 27
    6. Confirmation of Progress, 28
    7. Realization of the Goal, 29

i

V. SELF-CONFIDENCE: The Basis for Faith in God 33
    1. Prerequisite to Achievement, 33
    2. Faith in Self, Faith in God, 34
    3. A Formula for Success, 35
    4. Self-Realization, 36

VI. DISCIPLINE: Means to an End 39
    1. What Is Discipline? 39
    2. Benefits of Right Action, 40
    3. Our True Freedom, 41
    4. Key to a Productive Life, 41
    5. Maintain Discipline, 42
    6. Duties of a Devotee, 43
    7. Chart a Course, 44

VII. DHARMA AND DUTY: Right Action at Right Time 47
    1. Dharma: What Is It? 47
    2. How Do We Perform Our Dharma? 47
    3. A Role for Everyone, 48
    4. Like What You Have to Do, 49
    5. Your Heart Will Be Your Guide, 49
    6. Service: Responsibility to Society, 51
    7. Remember the Director of the Play, 52
    8. Duty to the Divine Self, 53

VIII. MORALITY: Foundation for Progress 57
    1. Religion Is Three-Fourths Character, 57
    2. What Is Morality? 58
    3. How We Can be Virtuous, 59
    4. Love: The Basis of Morality, 61

IX. SATSANG: Company of the Holy 63
    1. Why Seek Spiritual Company? 63
    2. What Is Good Company? 63
    3. We Adapt to Our Surroundings, 64
    4. Satsang, a Spiritual Discipline, 65
    5. Satsang or Socializing? 66
    6. Resolve to Seek Only the Good, 67

PART TWO: DEEPENING UNDERSTANDING

X. NAME: A Lantern in the Forest 69
    1. The Power of Words, 69
    2. Divine Names: Keys to Immortality, 70
    3. Namasmarana, a Practice for All, 71
    4. Say the Name with Feeling, 72
    5. Have Faith in God's Wisdom and Mercy, 73
    6. Regular Practice Grants Success, 73
    7. The Name Is Enough, 75

XI. PRAYER: Let's Talk 77
    1. Does Prayer Really Work? 77
    2. How Do We Start? 77
    3. What Should We Pray For? 79
    4. The Answer Comes When the Time Is Right, 81

XII. MEDITATION: Search for the Divinity Within 83
    1. What Is Meditation? 83
    2. How Do We Start? 84
    3. How Can We Recognize Progress? 86
    4. Make Joy Your Priceless Possession, 88

XIII. GRACE: How Sweet It Is 91
    1. What Is Grace? 91
    2. How Do We Get Grace? 91
    3. How Does Grace Appear? 94
    4. Without Grace, Nothing Starts or Finishes, 96

XIV. TRUTH: More Fundamental than the Atom 99
    1. The Unchanging Absolute, 99
    2. Can We Know Truth? 100
    3. How Do We Practice Truth? 100
    4. Love, the Highest Truth, 102

XV. NONDUALISM: Reflections of the Self 105
    1. The Basis of Unity, 105
    2. Why Does the One Appear as Many? 105
    3. God: With Form or Without Form? 107

4. "Atman Is Brahman," 108
5. How Can We Understand Nondualism? 109
6. Why Seek the Basis? 110

XVI. REINCARNATION: Here We Go Again 113
1. Evolution of the Soul, 113
2. Karma, Cause and Consequence, 114
3. Is Reincarnation Something New? 115
4. Why Do We Not Remember Past Lives? 116
5. Why Escape Rebirth? 117

XVII. KARMA: Action and Reaction 121
1. We Reap What We Sow, 121
2. How Do We Avoid Bad Karma? 123
3. Grace, the Most Effective Antidote, 124
4. The Best Course, 125
5. Karma Saves the Kitten, 127

XVIII. THE ATMA: Our Divine Nature 131
1. Know Thyself, 131
2. Atma, the God Within, 132
3. The Source of Understanding, 133
4. Realize Yourself and Be Free, 135

PART THREE. PRACTICING LOVE

XIX. LOVE: The Royal Road 139
1. The Basis of Creation, 139
2. How Do We Cultivate Love? 140
3. The Vision of Unity, 141
4. God Is Won by Love, 142

XX. SONG: Language of the Soul 145
1. Inspiration for the Journey, 145
2. The Song Meeting, 146
3. Standards: Musical or Devotional? 147
4. Take Up the Practice, 149

iv

XXI. MIRACLES: Outward Signs of Inner Events 151
    1. What Is a Miracle? 151
    2. Why Do Some Believe and Others Do Not? 151
    3. Why Does Sai Baba Perform Miracles? 152
    4. Natural Power, 155
    5. The Real Miracle, 156

XXII. NONVIOLENCE: Recognition of Kinship 159
    1. What Is Nonviolence? 159
    2. Violence Is Ignorance of Unity, 159
    3. The Role of Duty, 160
    4. Intention and Attitude, 163

XXIII. SUFFERING: Pain with a Purpose 165
    1. Our Cue to Move On, 165
    2. The Causes of Suffering, 165
    3. Tests of Character, 167
    4. An Opportunity for Growth, 168
    5. Nearness to God, 169

XXIV. SURRENDER: Fullness of Faith 173
    1. To Whom Do We Surrender? 173
    2. What Is Surrendered? 173
    3. Why Surrender? 174
    4. Surrender Must Be Complete, 175
    5. The Guards at the Gate, 176
    6. Expressway to Success, 177

XXV. PEACE: Oneness with God 181
    1. Virtue Is Peace, 181
    2. Our Real Nature, 182
    3. Inner Peace, Outer Peace, 183
    4. How Do We Cultivate Peace? 184

XXVI. DEVOTION: The Vision of Love 189
    1. What Is Devotion? 189
    2. The Path of Love, 189

3. Requisites for Success, 190
4. How to Start, 191
5. Perseverance Guarantees Accomplishment, 193
6. God, One Without Second, 193

XVII. SERVICE: A Gift of Love 197
    1. A Meaningful Contribution, 197
    2. Service to Self, 197
    3. Service as a Spiritual Discipline, 198
    4. Motivation for Service, 200
    5. Crossing the Ocean, 202

APPENDIX 205

ACKNOWLEDGMENTS

I am grateful to the many people who have helped to produce *Pathways to God*. I am particularly thankful for the support and practical assistance provided by the Tucson, Phoenix and Alameda study groups. Their experiences and suggestions have helped to make this volume truly useful for group discussions.

I owe a large measure of thanks also to my father, Simons Roof, for his highly valuable suggestions on both design and content. His great familiarity with the teachings of Vedanta and his professional writing experience have added an indispensable dimension to this volume. He and my mother, Marcia Moore, have my eternal gratitude for guiding my steps upon the Eastward path.

Much credit is also due to Andrea Gold and Meg Lundstrom for their editing skill and to Warren White for his efforts in arranging the final edition. Their contributions have been a great service.

FOREWORD

Newcomers to the Sai Baba centers often say: "Yes, I like the stories about Sai Baba, but what does he teach?"

This volume has been written primarily to answer this question. It was felt that a topical study guide with identified quotations would be a valuable aid to newcomers to the centers.

Many books are available which attempt to answer the question "Who is Sai Baba?" However, that question must ultimately be answered by each individual. Perhaps this study will help the reader to answer the question for himself or herself.

Twenty-seven major topics of spiritual study are discussed, with references for further research. The topics were chosen on the basis of their importance in Sai Baba's teachings and to provide a well-rounded course of spiritual study. The material covered should give the reader a foundation for further spiritual progress. Indeed, the teachings of Sathya Sai Baba provide an excellent course in Indian Vedanta even for the non-devotee.

A secondary purpose of *Pathways to God* is to provide material for the Sathya Sai study circle. The study circle is discussed in detail in the first chapter. It is hoped that the questions at the end of each chapter will provide the basis for lively discussion. Many times in the past, study circles have been conducted without proper guidelines and topics. Material has been needed which treats Indian spiritual concepts without undue use of difficult Sanskrit words. There has also been a lack of introductory material for English-speaking students. It is hoped that this volume will meet these needs.

In this study guide, quotations are identified to indicate their source in Sai Baba's writings or discourses. All quotations are from the words of Sathya Sai Baba unless otherwise indicated. The identification of quotations allows interested students to understand the context of what Sai Baba has said.

In addition, references for further study are provided at the end of each chapter. These references are identified by subject matter where single issues are raised; general discussions are not so identified. The

ix

bibliography at the end of the book identifies the volumes and editions used in preparation of Pathways of God. As editions may vary in page numbering, the page length of each volume is provided to help the student find the location of references.

Whether this guide is used for independent inquiry or by a study circle, it is hoped it will provide many benefits. It will, at least, give the student a good basic understanding of Indian spirituality. This volume should also assist the earnest student to tap his or her spiritual resources by illuminating the path ahead. It should promote integration of the personality and the blossoming of inner divinity. If the earnest pupil pursues the goal of God-realization, he or she should be richly rewarded in joyful love and self-fulfillment.

Author's Note

Minor spelling and grammatical changes have occasionally been made in quoted material. The purpose is simply to keep all quotations and the general text consistent with standard editorial practice and to avoid any possible confusion of understanding and usage on the part of readers.

Part One: The Journey Begins

CHAPTER ONE

Study Circle: A Tool for Transformation

1. How Spiritual Training Begins

An ounce of honest doubt and a commitment to self-improvement are the only requirements for beginning the spiritual journey. When we first set foot on the path, our only assurance of success lies in our sincere inquiry. Faith, devotion, and knowledge grow in time, but an open mind is required for their development. Earnest seekers will find that a harvest of joy awaits them when they cultivate the field of divinity.

Spiritual growth needs to be approached along several avenues. Devotion, study, and service are especially required. Study alone cannot carry us to God-realization: our knowledge must be seasoned with devotion to win the Lord's grace. Similarly, devotion without study and service limits our realization of our full spiritual potential. A balanced approach to the spiritual life promises the best results.

The Sathya Sai Baba study circle promotes an integrated approach to spiritual endeavor. Practice and sincerity are held in higher esteem than voluminous knowledge. Experience and devotion are given greater credence than academic learning. The study circle seeks to transform our behavior -- not to fill our heads with undigested information. It conveys practical knowledge that uplifts and ennobles our characters. Only the process of character-building can be called true education.

Not information, but transformation; not instruction, but construction should be the aim. Theoretical knowledge is a burden unless it is practiced, for then it can be lightened into wisdom and assimiliated into daily life. Knowledge that does not give harmony and wholeness to the process of living is not worth acquiring. Every activity must be rendered valid and worthwhile by its contribution to the discovery of truth, both of the self and of nature.

Sathya Sai Speaks 9, p. 51

2. The Study Circle's Purpose

The study circle is a human dynamo that charges us with ideas, inspiration, and resolve. It lifts the weary and points the way when we become lost. The discipline pushes us from behind as it holds a light in front to guide us. The process is simple, but the results can be wondrous.

A study circle is a group of aspirants who meet regularly to discuss spiritual topics. A group leader coordinates the discussion, giving each participant an opportunity to present his or her view of the current subject. The study circle is not a debate. Members are encouraged to state their views, but are discouraged from criticizing others' views. A variety of perspectives is sought on a common theme. During the course of the discussion, the group leader attempts to summarize major themes and to develop a consensus on the important points.

> *Hislop asked the question, "What is study circle?" It is not just reading books. "Circle, study circle" means taking a point and each person discussing what is the meaning of the point to them -- like a roundtable conference. Each person gives his point of view, and finally values are derived from this. If there is just reading, there is doubt. But if each one gives his view, doubts will be answered. The topic is viewed; the study circle looks at different facets. It is like a diamond with its different facets, but there is one facet that is flat, the top facet, and from this all can be viewed. To discover the top facet is the task of the study circle.*
>
> *Conversations, pp. 125-126*

The study circle enables us to learn from the wisdom of saints and sages through quotations and references, and also from our peers. The sacred scriptures of all lands may be consulted as sources of wisdom, but in discussing spiritual topics with our contemporaries, we interpret behavior appropriate to our own time and culture. The newcomer benefits from hearing the views of those with more experience. Experienced members gain by restating and clarifying their views. Participants who find book study difficult profit from the discussion, while the studious learn from the practical comments of those with a less academic and more service-oriented bent. In each case the aspirant is encouraged to make a systematic habit of study and practice.

3. Knowledge and Self-Confidence

A rose blossoms in the pure sunlight. With proper food, water, and care, it grows full and tall. The study circle provides us with similar benefits. With the care of every member, it grants the pure light of inspiration, the food of knowledge, and the water of self-confidence. Through regular discussion and study, we build confidence in our knowledge -- and perhaps even acquire some wisdom. We clarify our ideas and learn to express our views on spiritual topics. We learn to listen more closely to others' ideas and to consider other viewpoints. By fellow aspirants, we are inspired to regularly practice spiritual disciplines.

Subjects for discussion usually differ from session to session. Questions or quotations based on general themes, such as those contained in this book, can create the basis for excellent discussions. The spiritual questions or concerns of members also provide good subjects. If a member is experiencing difficulty with a point of study or practice, it may be beneficial for him or her to discuss the subject in a study circle. Usually, if one member has questions, others will have the same question.

Authoritative texts, such as the *Bhagavad Gita* or Swami's published discourses, are sometimes chosen for systematic study because they cover a variety of pertinent topics. Whatever theme is chosen, it is best to maintain some flexibility in the discussion. Related issues may be aired without drifting too far from the original subject. If the group chooses a topic in advance each week, members may research the theme before discussion. This tends to create a more rewarding exchange because members arrive prepared with thoughts and quotations on the topic.

4. A Typical Study Circle Routine

Study circles will inevitably vary in some respects. Each group of aspirants radiates its own distinctive light, and so each group adopts an approach that suits its needs. However, some aspects of the circle should remain fairly constant.

A study circle should meet regularly, weekly if possible. The location should be convenient for all members. Every participant should be welcome, for each is a valuable part of the group. In study circles, as in other center functions, Swami asks that men and women sit on separate sides of the circle. This helps all participants to concentrate on the subject at hand. Only at public functions, where outside guests are invited, does Swami relax this rule.

Swami says there is no specific limit on how many may participate in the circle. However, the size of the room available and the time allotted may require certain prearrangements. More than one circle may be conducted if many participants are present. This is particularly true if all members cannot meet at one location or at one time. Differences of interest may also necessitate the presentation of themes of particular relevence to groups within a center. For example, a group of parents may wish to focus on issues related to child-rearing. A limit of forty-five minutes to one hour allows sufficient time for a discussion without it becoming tiresome.

A successful study format begins with a short presentation by the week's leader. This presentation may last from five to fifteen minutes, depending on the subject matter. Complex, research-oriented topics take longer to present than subjects of general knowledge. The purpose of the introduction is to highlight the important themes of the subject. This allows participants to focus on the subject, particularly if they have been unable to read previously the passage under discussion. An introduction also starts to generate ideas for discussion when the subject is opened to members' comments. It is desirable for the presentation to include various viewpoints and to conclude with a question for discussion. Quotations with apparent contradictions frequently stimulate discussion. After a question is posed, a one- or two-minute meditation allows participants to collect their thoughts before speaking.

Rotation of the leader's task affords each member an opportunity to research and prepare for a meeting. All regular participants are encouraged to present a topic, but they should not be required to do so.

5. Suggested "Rules"

Rivers aid us in food production, transportation, and recreation, but they are only helpful when they remain within their banks. If they overflow their bounds, they can cause untold destruction. For aspirants, rules are the banks which make our efforts productive. In the study circle, it is important that all participants be aware of the "rules" from the start. Rules may vary in detail, but some guidelines should be maintained for a productive discussion. Nine rules to encourage active participation are suggested below.

1. The meeting should be started with omkar (the repetition of Om three times) and a prayer or spiritual song to raise the atmosphere of the meeting room. This creates a climate of brotherhood and cooperation among all participants and a feeling of working toward a common goal. If the study circle occurs after a devotional song meeting, it is not necessary to sing additional songs.

2. The study circle is not a debating society; it is an exploration of viewpoints. Each participant should feel free to speak without fear of judgment or personal criticism.

3. Active and equal participation should be sought from all members. The facilitator of the discussion may need to encourage new members to speak. New or quiet members often require a break in the conversation to present their views, and will not speak if another participant appears ready to speak.

4. Dominant members must take care not to monopolize the conversation. A time limit may be placed on individual comments to deter enthusiastic members from "lecturing" the group. However, tact and courtesy should be used by the facilitator in observing this rule.

5. The discussion leader and members should avoid reading long quotations. The study circle is not a reading club. Lengthy quotations often prove tiring. It is particularly inappropriate to read long passages in foreign languages which other members do not understand.

6. Each group member should be engaged in turn. This is done by taking turns, with members speaking in a circular order. Although reticent members should be encouraged to speak, they should not be required to do so. They may elect to pass and perhaps comment after all others have taken their turns.

7. Quotations or anecdotes should be relevant to the topic. Quotations particularly should be chosen from sources which all members would consider authoritative. In the Sai Baba study circle, the most appropriate quotations are from the discourses and writings of Sathya Sai Baba.

8.   A moderator should be named in advance for one or more discussion sessions. It is that person's duty to see that participants follow study circle guidelines. The moderator is responsible for helping the group adhere to the meeting format and for keeping the discussion moving. The moderator for the week need not be the person presenting the topic.

9.   A single specific question should be posed to the group for discussion. It should concern a practical aspect of spiritual life. In small circles, more than one question may be posed if time allows. It is helpful to take several minutes of reflection on the question before starting the discussion.

If these guidelines are followed, the study circle should proceed well. Above all, members must feel welcomed and that their views are regarded as valuable. Respect all participants and encourage them to speak, for each has a special viewpoint to share.

6. The Goal of Self-Discovery

Self-discovery fills us with joy and confidence. It fulfills our expectations and grants us spiritual satisfaction. It is the prize which encourages us to further effort. Through the discipline of the study circle, we learn to visualize the goal of our efforts. Equipped with greater knowledge, our practice and devotion both benefit. With inspiration and incentive from the group, we strive to advance in self-understanding. In such an atmosphere of loving cooperation, each of us progresses closer to the goal of discovering the vast potential within. The honest doubt with which we began the journey gives way to a joyous knowledge as we experience the truth of ourselves.

CHAPTER TWO

Organization: A Structure For Growth

1. Why a Sai Organization?

The question is sometimes asked: "What is the need of a Sai Baba organization?" Many spiritual and service groups already dot the map of human endeavor. If transpersonal growth is largely a personal matter, why create an organization?

The structure created by Sathya Sai Baba is unique. It is a forum where aspirants learn spiritual values. It is a training ground where members practice service to others. It is a temple of devotion and an instrument for the transformation of society. The primary objective of the Sai organization, however, is to aid seekers in their quest for God by helping them to recognize the divinity in all.

> *There are thousands of organizations already working with such aims, but what is the special need for an organization bearing my name? You must realize me in all, and serve all in a spirit of worshipful dedication.*
>
> *Sathya Sai Speaks 6, pp. 323-324*

Members of the Sai Baba centers are encouraged to awaken to universal divinity. When all people and objects are seen as reflections of God, peace and brotherhood will shine on Earth. Fear and conflict result from the illusion of separateness. That illusion is produced when the divine vision is reflected on an impure heart.

> *The organization must help people to realize the unity behind all this apparent multiplicity, which is only a superimposition by the human mind on the One that is all this.*
>
> *Sathya Sai Speaks 10, p. 45*

To realize divinity in others, we must first uncover the light within ourselves. We must believe that the divine spark which motivates us also resides in others. The Sai organization seeks to purify the individual's heart and mind. Service, study, and devotional singing all contribute to accomplishing this result. In the company of like-minded aspirants, the member is encouraged to progress on the path. The organization's objective is the transformation of the individual. If enough individuals are transformed, then perhaps the problems of society will diminish also.

> I must say plainly that ninety out of a hundred among you have not clearly visualized the purpose for which I have allowed you to form these organizations...It is to build upon the earth the fatherhood of God and the brotherhood of men on strong foundations. This must be clearly grasped by all of you. You are not engaged in social service through these organizations; you are engaged in your own service. All the items of work are aimed at expanding your heart and purifying it.
>
> *Sathya Sai Speaks 6, p. 321*

2. Rules, Timely Suggestions

The primary qualifications for membership in the Sai organization are sincerity, faith, and virtue. We need not have wealth, position, or formal education, but we must strive sincerely to experience our own truth. We must have faith in God and in our ability to achieve self-realization.

> For example, who can be members of these organizations, and what are their qualifications? (1) Of course, they must be eager aspirants for spiritual progress. (2) They must have full faith in the name that the organization bears and in spreading that name in the manner suited to its message and majesty. (3) Besides, the member must have won recognition as a good person. That is all the qualification needed; nothing else counts.
>
> *Sathya Sai Speaks 6, p. 36*

Rules and qualifications are kept to a bare minimum, however the Sathya Sai Organization in America has formulated a number of guidelines for the smooth operation of the centers. These suggested policies have been derived from the long experience of member directors and officers. As such, they should be carefully considered and implemented in the great majority of cases. Still, there is a recognition that individual situations may arise where the spiritual creativity of locally selected officers will find an original solution. Sathya Sai Baba usually does not inist on one solution, preferring instead to allow for some flexibility in achieving objectives.

> *Avatars seldom give advice directly. Whatever they wish to communicate, they convey more often by way of indirect suggestions and only rarely by the direct method of instruction. The reason for this is there is divinity inherent in every human being, which he can manifest spontaneously, if favorable conditions are provided, just as a viable seed will germinate and grow into a tree because of its inherent nature, if only suitable facilities are provided for the manifestation of its potentiality. Man should be enabled to correct himself by his own efforts, by merely giving kindly suggestions, rather than by stultifying his freedom and dignity through directives imposed from without.*

Indian Culture and Spirituality, pp. 95-96

Our efforts in building the Sathya Sai Organization need to be first directed inward, so that we may understand the goals of spiritual endeavor. Only when our own lives are in order can we help others. Once we express a pure divine vision others will come to share the joy that we have found. As messengers of Sai our aim must be to implement the rules in a spirit of loving cooperation.

> *Note that there are three classes of messengers: those who do not understand the orders of the master or do not care to understand, and those who operate to the detriment of the work assigned to them; those who do only just as much as the order literally communicates; and those who grasp the purpose and significance of the orders and carry them out unflinchingly until the purpose is achieved.*

Sathya Sai Speaks 10, p. 89

An effective organization is unable to function without any regulations. Some people chafe at rules and will not participate in an organization which sets certain prescribed limitations. However, rules are the guideposts which point the way and mold members into better people. They are the obligations of membership, which each of us accepts when we enter the Sai fold.

> *The restrictions, rules and self-controls are the royal road leading to the goal of self-realization. They are not just to bind you, to limit or control you.*

Seva Dal, Feb. 81, p. 8

When we accept the benefits of a spiritual path, we must also maintain the integrity and discipline of that path. The rules of the Sai organization emphasize sincerity and practice of Swami's teachings. If we do not adhere to the rules, we harm ourselves and also others. Like a careless driver, the undisciplined member is a hazard to self and those nearby.

> *Our rules emphasize that members must first practice what they stand for. Whatever you desire others to do, you must first put into daily practice sincerely and with steadfastness.*
> *Sathya Sai Speaks 6, p. 35*

Before we apply for membership or office in the Sai organization, we must consider well the requirements and obligations. Membership forges a special and direct link to Sathya Sai Baba. It requires sincerity and constant effort. The motive for membership must not be for recognition or exercise of power. Only the highest ideals can justify the bond of membership.

> *Before you enter the organization or seek any office therein, consider well whether you have the yearning and the capacity; else, if you join and complain against some person or some program, you are only revealing your own smallness or weakness. Make due inquiry, give full consideration, before you join the organization. Having joined, cooperate with others vigorously and carry out all your duties conscientiously.*
> *Sathya Sai Speaks 7, p. 329*

3. Duties and Responsibilities of Officers

Of paramount importance in the Sai organization is the role of center officers. Those who speak for the organization must lead lives which are an example to others. They are watched closely and their lead is taken more often than they know. It is not appopriate for them to adhere to other teachings and practices that do not conform to the ideals laid down by Sai. Usually it is acceptable for ministers of traditional religions to be officers of a Sai center, however, such representatives must be careful not to mislead those who follow. If they adhere to teachings which are not consistent which Sai's message, they should not serve as officers.

> *It is also laid down strictly that those who are in our organization should not have any connection with other organizations of spiritual or religious character...Though people can revere and worship whomsoever they like, we*

*should not have in the organization men with dual loyalties.
Only those with faith and devotion in this name and form
can carry out its objectives with zest and enthusiasm.*
Sathya Sai Speaks 7, p. 343

Officers most follow closely the guidelines and code of conduct laid down by Sai. If they are unable to do so, they should not hold office. Office signifies service to others, not lordship over them. By their service, officers must demonstrate humility and spur them members onto greater effort.

*Office bearers cannot claim any privilege or exemption.
They must evince leadership; by their devotion and faith,
they must inspire the waverers. That is their function.*
Sathya Sai Speaks 7, p. 166

Selection of officers is not based on popularity or length of service; the important factor is whether the nominee leads a good life and is able to properly administer the affairs of the center. Faith, humility, devotion, service, and love towards all are the primary requisites. An officer who is attached to power or ego fulfillment is a positive danger to the center.

*So the very first ideal you must keep in mind when you start
and run these organizations is: do not crave for status or
authority or position; do not allow any pomp or show; do not
compete for publicity or for recognition or for praise.*
Sathya Sai Speaks 6, p. 32

The method of choosing officers is referred to as "selection." Officers should be selected by the unanimous decision of the membership after thoughtful discussion. Adjustments to center policy or programs should be acted upon openly and with careful consideration prior to selection of officers. Center policy should not hinge on the will of the officer in charge at the time. A situation where all members cannot agree on leadership or policy signifies deeper problems. It indicates the exercise of ego and attachment to personal goals.

4. A Call to Action

The opportunity to learn and to serve is a priceless treasure. Work within the Sai center is a chance for devotional practice of a high order. It provides a field for reducing the ego and serving selflessly.

The benefits are incalculable. Membership forges a close bond to Sathya Sai Baba. That relationship provides us with an unparalleled opportunity for spiritual progress. If we dive into that sea, we can obtain the treasure which it holds. It is useless to stand at the shore and proclaim that the sea holds no riches. Only if we work with the highest ideals and dedication can we secure the prize.

Questions for Study Circle

1. What is the purpose of a Sai Baba organization?
2. Who establishes the rules in the Sai organization?
3. Can we achieve our spiritual goals just as well without being members of the organization?
4. Does the organization have a role in trying to reform society?
5. How are officers selected?
6. What are the duties of officers?
7. What are the duties of members?
8. Does the organization have a role in setting standards of behavior for members?
9. How are differences of opinion on administrative matters handled in the center?
10. What are the potential benefits of membership?

References for Further Study

1. Conversations, p. 85.
2. Sathya Sai Speaks 6, pp. 33-41, 158-159.
3. Sathya Sai Speaks 7, pp. 164-173.
4. Sathya Sai Speaks 7, p. 171 (Members benefit from holding office in rotation).
5. Sathya Sai Speaks 7, pp. 336-345, 359-372.
6. Sathya Sai Speaks 9, p. 12 (The transformation of individuals and society).

7. Sathya Sai Speaks 10, pp. 43-47.

8. Sathya Sai Speaks 11, p. 37 (The organization must cultivate unity).

9. Spiritual Directives/Advice on Operation of Sai Centers (A compilation by J. Jagadeesan).

10. Summer Showers 1974, p. 210 (Leaders must practice what they know).

CHAPTER THREE

The Avatar: Light From Above

1. What Is an Avatar?

The word *avatar* is derived from the Sanskrit word meaning "descent." An avatar is a descent of spirit into form. Although all people are spiritual beings encased in mortal bodies, the word *avatar* describes the manifestation of God in human form. All people possess a divine inner reality, but few manifest it. The avatar expresses divinity throughout his incarnation. His earthly career is a sign of his everlasting love for all people.

> *Generally, the avatar is described as a "coming down" from a higher status to a lower one. But no! When the baby in the cradle weeps, wails, and clamors for help, the mother stoops and takes it in her arms. Her stoop is not to be described as a "coming down."*
>
> *Sathya Sai Speaks 10, p. 229*

2. When Darkness Threatens

In the Hindu tradition, the Supreme Godhead is said to incarnate from age to age when evil is rampant and righteousness is in danger of extinction. He comes to reestablish justice and spiritual order. By an act of divine will, he assumes a human form to reverse the trend of social decline.

> *Whenever there is a languishing of dharma (spiritual duty) or righteousness and an upheaval of unrighteousness, I create myself, for it is part of the primal resolution, or sankalpa, to protect the spiritual structure of the universe. I lay aside my formless essence and assume a name and a form suited to the purpose for which I come. Whenever evil threatens to vanquish good, I have to come and save it from decline.*
>
> *Sathya Sai Speaks 5, p. 324*

The Lord takes human birth to save the good and subdue evil-doers. When evil threatens to overwhelm righteousness and devotees pray for redemption, the Lord incarnates to renew the path of spiritual endeavor. The call of earnest aspirants draws the Lord to manifest himself. Their prayers and his compassion culminate in this epochal event.

> *The Lord comes as avatar when he is anxiously awaited by saints and sages. Sadhus prayed -- and I have come.*
>
> *Sathya Sai Speaks 4, p. 8*

The Lord takes birth to show us the means to achieve God-realization. Only by appearing as a human being can he illustrate correct paths of action. Only by living among us can he encourage aspirants to understand and love God. We require an example to demonstrate divine qualities.

> *This formless being comes in the form of a human being so that he may mix with the human beings and set up examples and ideals for human beings and convey to them all aspects that they should learn.*
>
> *Summer Roses on the Blue Mountains, p. 51*

By assuming human form, the Lord sets an example of ideal human behavior. By appearing among us, he captures our love and motivates us to action. The epic tales of ancient India (the *Mahabharata*, the *Ramayana*, and the *Puranas)* recount the lives of the avatars such as Rama and Krishna in past ages. These accounts are not simply histories: they are guidebooks of spiritual living. They set forth ideal examples of right conduct, compassion, and truth. They illustrate the tender and "human" side of God as well as his might.

> *The Avatara behaves in a human way so that mankind can feel kinship, but rises to superhuman heights so that mankind can aspire to those heights.*
>
> *Sathya Sai Speaks 4, p. 41*

The reasons for God to incarnate in each age vary in detail. The manifestation must suit the time and circumstance. Some incarnations appear for a specific and limited purpose. Other avatars come for more general reasons, such as reestablishing truth and spiritual direction.

Of the avatars, some are for a definite limited purpose, like Vamana or Narasimha. They are just manifestations to counter some particular evils. They are not full-fledged, long-lasting, expansive, like Rama and Krishna.

Sathya Sai Speaks 4, p. 154

For this reason, some incarnations are born with only the powers requisite for the task at hand. Others, such as Sathya Sai, are endowed with powers beyond the immediate need. The Rama avatar manifested part of his power through his brothers. However, Krishna was a poorna (full) avatar, an incarnation manifesting complete divine powers.[1]

That is to say, the avatar might manifest only such part of the Divine Glory as was essential for the task which brought the form or it might exceed the limited purpose for which it came and shine in full grandeur. Rama is a good example of the first and Krishna of the second.

Sathya Sai Speaks 4, p. 132

The goal of the avatar suits the requirements of the age. During the four spiritual ages of humanity, the message is taught according to human capacity to learn. In the Kritha Yuga, the spiritual "Golden Age," meditation was emphasized. In the Treta Yuga, the following era, ritual acts and sacrifices held primary importance. In the declining Dwapara Yuga, ritual worship dominated spiritual endeavor. In the current age, the Kali Yuga, which is characterized by spiritual decline, the principal lesson is simply remembrance of the name of the Lord.[2] The Kali Yuga commenced at the time of Krishna's death, February 20, 3102 B.C.[3] It will have a duration of 11,000 years.[4]

It is not possible for human beings to fully understand the nature of the avatar. Although he appears as a human being, his power and capacity soar beyond our understanding. He sees the past, present, and future of all. By his unique powers, he guides individuals and society toward spiritual regeneration.

---

1. *Sathya Sai Speaks 4, pg. 164*
2. *Summer Showers 1978, pg. 8*
3. *Conversations, pg. 20*
4. *Summer Roses on the Blue Mountain, pg. 90*

The avatara-purusha, however, has come solely to save mankind, and so he is aware of the pilgrim, the path, and the goal. He is the Master of Creation and he is fully conscious of his power. He knows the past, the present, and the future of all. He leads and liberates.

Sathya Sai Speaks 7, p. 473

3. The Nature of the Avatar

Although the avatar wields power beyond imagination, he relates to each of us as our closest friend. He reads the heart and mind of each. To each man, woman, or child, he appears not as a powerful sovereign, but as our dearest companion. His power manifests to us as love and wisdom, not as force or dominion.

The avatar is a child to the children, a boy to the boys, a man among men, a woman among women, so that the avatar's message might reach each heart and receive enthusiastic response as ananda (bliss). It is the compassion of the avatar that prompts his every activity.

Sathya Sai Speaks 7, p. 275

The history of India is resonant with the traditions of the avatars and of great saints. In India, spiritual realization is considered to be the pinnacle of human achievement. It is a testimony to the spiritual greatness of India that poorna avatars are incarnated only in that land.[5] It is a land replete with the language and the teachings of divinity. However, even in India it is not easy for human beings to recognize an avatar. Rama and Krishna were recognized as divine by very few people in their times. Despite the transcendental greatness of those days, even family and kin did not recognize the divinity of these incarnations.

The incarnations of the Lord were not accepted as such by many. Even their parents, kinsmen, and comrades hesitated to adore them. Only a few sages who had cultivated the inner vision through study and sadhana knew their reality.

Sathya Sai Speaks 6, p. 333

---

5.   *Conversations, pg. 121*

Lack of recognition resulted partly because Rama and Krishna were born into royal families. They were not available to the public, nor did they announce their missions. The avatars of old were only recognized by the masses after they dropped their physical forms.

On previous occasions when God incarnated on earth, the bliss of recognizing him in the incarnation was vouchsafed only after the physical embodiment had left the world, in spite of plenty of patent evidences of his grace. And the loyalty and devotion they commanded from men arose through fear and awe at their superhuman powers and skills, or at their imperial and penal authority.

Sathya Sai Speaks 6, p. 212

4. How to Recognize the Divine Being

To recognize an avatar, we must have some enlightened perception. How much more difficult the task has become in this age of spiritual decline! People believe that God will manifest in a form suitable to their preconceptions, if they even consider the possibility of divine incarnations. Today, people's images of divinity are drawn from history books whose information is not appropriate to this age. So when the Lord arrives, we must look to the example, the signs, and the teaching.

Many are drawn away by the outer signs of sainthood: the long gown, the beard, the rosaries, the matted hair. They keep track of many such who move about in this land and follow them into the wilderness. It is very difficult to demarcate clearly the manifestation of the Lord, and so I am announcing myself, and am myself describing my mission, the task, the characteristics, the qualities which mark out the avatar from the rest.

Sathya Sai Speaks 4, p. 21

The ancient teachings of India offer some hints on how to discern an avatar. They say that an avatar is recognized by certain attributes. The more attributes possessed, the greater the scope of the incarnation. The greatest avatars possess power over the sixteen "activities." The first fifteen attributes involve mastery over physical functions, the senses, and the elements. They are described in various ways to illustrate the avatar's power over the physical elements. The sixteenth attribute is universal omniscience, omnipotence, and omnipresence. This power is held only by poorna (full) avatars.[6] Poorna avatars incarnate very rarely; the last historical poorna avatar was Krishna, who lived approximately five thousand years ago.

Certain physical signs also point to the appearance of an avatar. These appear as marks on the left side of the body. The eagle-shaped birthmark on the chest, the garuda, is such a sign. Another is the wheel-shaped mark on the sole of the foot.[7] Additional signs may be foretold in prophecy.

5. How to Benefit from the Incarnation

For aspirants whose intuitive vision is open, this is a time of great opportunity. The poorna avatar of the Kali Yuga is now incarnate as Sri Sathya Sai Baba. He has come possessed of the sixteen attributes and the physical signs foretold in past ages. He manifests the energy and powers of a superhuman being, yet some observers are still unsure of his stature. On occasion, he pretends not to know the visitor or where the visitor comes from, but that is his play. The devotee must overcome the illusion which blinds him to the magnificent reality.

> Since I move about with you, eat like you, and talk with you, you are deluded into the belief that this is but an instance of common humanity. Be warned against this mistake. I am also deluding you by my singing with you, talking with you, and engaging myself in activities with you. But any moment my divinity may be revealed to
>
> you; you have to be ready, prepared for that moment. Since divinity is enveloped by humanness, you must endeavor to overcome the maya (delusion) that hides it from your eyes.
>
> *Sathya Sai Speaks 6, p. 211*

In this age, the avatar has come to reestablish righteousness and the sacred teachings. There is now no single great enemy of humanity; there

---

6.   *Conversations, pg. 73*

7.   *Vision of the Divine, pg. 12*

is both good and evil in all. And so he comes to educate and uplift all of humanity.

> *In past ages, avatars rid the world of evil by destroying the few fanatics and ogres who wrought it. But now fanaticism and felony reign in every heart...Therefore everyone needs correction; everyone has to be educated and guided in the right path.*
>
> *Sathya Sai Speaks 4, p. 3*

Even now the mission moves forward. The message is clear for all to see. Aspirants need only examine the teachings to benefit from the lesson. Sathya Sai Baba is the guide and example for the Kali Age. It is up to each of us to walk the path. Only thus will humanity be saved from the precipice of disaster.

> *The way in which the avatar has to be used for one's liberation and uplift is: watch his every step, observe his actions and activities, follow the guiding principle of which his life is an elaboration. Mark his love, his compassion, his wisdom; try to bring them into your own life.*
>
> *Sathya Sai Speaks 6, pp. 166-167*

By observing the Lord and capturing his grace, we can win the goal of liberation. The Lord himself will guide us. His task is the deliverance of those who are ready for liberation from the cycle of birth and death. If this opportunity is lost, when will another chance come?

> *The airplane has to land at certain places in order to take in those who have won the right to fly by the tickets they have purchased. So, too, the Lord has to come*
>
> *down so that those who have won the right to be liberated may be saved; incidentally, others too will know of the Lord, of his grace, of ways of winning it, of the joy of liberation.*
>
> *Sathya Sai Speaks 4, p. 24*

The avatar has come to light the lamp of love. His words illumine the heart and soul. But first one small task is required: we must open the door so that the light and the joy may enter.

The incarnation comes to warn, to guide, to awaken, to lay down the path and shed the light of love on it. But man has to listen, learn, and obey with hope and faith.

Sathya Sai Speaks 8, p. 143

Questions for Study Circle

1. Why does God take a physical form?

2. How do we recognize an avatar?

3. Why are some avatars endowed with full divine powers while others are not?

4. Do avatars incarnate often enough?

5. Why do avatars not change dire situations immediately by use of their powers?

6. How much of the avatar's mission can we understand?

7. Why are poorna avatars born only in India?

8. What gifts does the avatar offer us in this era?

9. If you were the avatar, what would you do?

References for Further Study

1. Conversations, pp. 116-117 (Recognizing an avatar).

2. Gita Vahini, pp. 65-66.

3. My Baba and I, pp. 17-18 (Signs of an avatar).

4. Sathya Sai Speaks 1, p. 191 (Seven characteristics).

5. Sathya Sai Speaks 2, p. 131.

6. Sathya Sai Speaks 4, Chapter 12.

7. Sathya Sai Speaks 4, pp. 187-188 (Why the Lord himself comes to save humanity).

8. Sathya Sai Speaks 6, p. 66.

9. Sathya Sai Speaks 7, p. 182 (Dates of Kali Yuga).

10. Sathya Sai Speaks 8, p. 109 (Mission of avatar in each age).

11. Sathya Sai Speaks 8, p. 144 (Relationship between Sai Baba and Jesus).

12. Sathya Sai Speaks 9, p. 107 (Krishna avatar fostered love).

13. Sathya Sai Speaks 10, p. 230 (Jesus was a Karana-Janma).

14. Summer Showers 1974, pp. 276-290 (Who Sai is).

15. Summer Showers 1977, p. 5 (God comes to set ideal examples).

16. Summer Showers 1977, p. 27 (Reasons for Rama avatar).

17. Summer Showers 1979, pp. 48-49.

18. Vidya Vahini, p. 27 (Avatars can confer spiritual strength).

19. Vision of the Divine, pp. 12-13 (The signs and powers of avatars).

CHAPTER FOUR

Faith: The Source of Knowledge

1. All People Have Some Faith

Nothing is accomplished without faith. We must have faith in ourselves or in others to complete any task. We must have faith in the laws of nature. We must have faith that we will live to see the results of right effort. So also we must have faith in God if we are to make spiritual progress. Faith is the first step that makes each following step possible.

> Faith is the basis of every act. You do not run away from the barber because he is armed with a sharp razor. You place faith in him and allow him to cut your hair, quietly submitting to his idiosyncrasies. You give away costly clothes to the washer since you have faith that he will return them washed and ironed...So, too, believe in the inner motivator, the atman within, the voice of God.
>
> *Sathya Sai Speaks 10, pp. 227-228*

2. The Origin of Belief

Faith springs from self-understanding. It is inner divinity that enables us to recognize divinity in the world. That internal source is a spring of courage and self-confidence. It swells into a river as it flows back into the sea of understanding, for we are only seeking to regain our lost inheritance -- divinity.

> For what is the root of that faith in yourself? Who are you that you should believe in yourself? No. You believe in yourself because your self is God and you have an unshakable faith in God, deep down in you. Faith in yourself and faith in God are identical; you tap the strength of the God within when you stand at attention against an enemy without.
>
> *Sathya Sai Speaks 2, p. 229*

Some faith comes naturally to us. If we must submit to an operation, we believe that the surgeon will save us, despite the sharp knife in the surgeon's hand. We believe that oncoming highway traffic will remain in its own lane of travel. We have confidence in complete strangers, but to place faith in God makes us more critical. We have a tendency to believe what is pleasant and easy. It is more difficult to believe when faith demands action or obligation. Faith in God presents an array of challenges to the newcomer. It frequently requires major changes in the new believer's lifestyle. However, without faith in the messages of the saints and sages, effective progress is impossible.

> You may say that you will not believe in God unless you have clear experience personally about him. Well, you believe that your date of birth is a certain month in a particular year. You have taken it on trust. You take many things on trust: it is impossible to insist on personal experience for everything which we have to believe, if life is to run smooth. Take this also on trust, for many saints, sages, and scientists have accepted it and experienced it.
>
> Sathya Sai Speaks 7, p. 311

Knowledge arises from experience, but first we must act on faith. We must act to win the experience that rewards faith. If we test the instructions given by others who have gone before, we will discover for ourselves the "hidden" riches. It is not proper to demand proof of the existence of God before any effort is expended. Great trouble is endured to achieve material objectives, but some people feel that the greater aim of spiritual growth should be effortless. If such individuals do not make the effort, the loss is their own.

> Some people say that they will believe in God only when they are afforded some experience of divine will. How can faith arise in the will for those with such an attitude? They have no keenness to experience; how can examples help? Of course, if some have no faith, the loss is theirs. The Lord is unconcerned. Two and two make four even if some swear that they will not believe it.
>
> Sathya Sai Speaks 6, p. 110

3. The Necessity of Faith

Even the enjoyment of a happy life in the world requires faith. We must believe in an intelligent guiding force, or the world is reduced to a chaotic jungle of greed and envy. Life is not pleasant for one caught in the coils of self-importance and wrong desire. Without concern for others, there is little joy in life. Lasting joy is found only when we aspire to universal values and ideals.

But spiritual progress is not merely intellectual exercise: it is right living, good conduct, moral behavior. These attitudes are the automatic consequence of belief in a good, just, compassionate God who is watching and witnessing every act. So faith in an omnipresent, omniscient, omnipotent God is the first prerequisite to a good life.

Sathya Sai Speaks 6, p. 108

4. Guard the Tender Shoots

Without faith, where can happiness be found? At first the work is difficult and the results are not readily apparent. But with time, faith blossoms into a tree under which many find shade. One step at a time is sufficient for even the longest journey. It is not necessary to finish the journey in one day. At the beginning we need to guard faith, as a small flame must be guarded from the wind.

When faith dawns, fence it around with discipline and self-control so that the tender shoot might be guarded against goats and cattle, the motley crowd of cynics and unbelievers. When your faith grows into a big tree, those very cattle can lie down in the shade that it will spread.

Sathya Sai Speaks 1, pp. 37-38

Until faith is strong, it is best for us to remain silent. By challenging others, we may lose the little faith we have. When faith is unshakable, we can aid others. Firm faith is like a raging fire: it will consume even the green wood of others' doubts. Until that time, silence is the kindest friend of faith.

Faith is a plant of slow growth; its roots go deep into the heart. Silence is the best sadhana (spiritual practice) to guard faith.

Sathya Sai Speaks 5, p. 68

5. The Road to Victory

With steady, faithful effort, victory is assured. A disciplined approach yields the most fruitful results. We must persist despite setbacks and obstacles. When our practice conforms to our precept and the Lord's grace is won, the prize will be awarded.

Steady faith alone can earn victory. You cannot be changing your allegiance as and when you please. Hold fast until the realization is awarded.

Sathya Sai Speaks 5, p. 73

The faith with which we pursue the goal helps to implement the result. The Lord rewards faith with grace. He is so compassionate that he will not disappoint the earnest seeker. The certainty of our expectation is like the force of a great wave -- it sweeps away all obstacles in its path.

Faith can work wonders: it can compel the Lord to manifest himself and give you what you believe he will give you.

Sathya Sai Speaks 2, p. 216

Unshakable faith does not grow overnight. It arrives on a slow cart, pulled by the oxen of strength and determination. There can be no more worthy object of effort than realizing the omnipresent God. Our faith grants us patience while we develop spiritual discrimination. Spiritual discrimination enables us to know what is real and of lasting value. When we taste the sweetness of spiritual values, the journey becomes a pleasure. Until that time, faith sustains the vision.

That faith can come only slowly, by association with the godly, by reading the lives and experiences of godly persons, and by gaining experience oneself.

Sathya Sai Speaks 7, p. 124

6. Confirmation of Progress

The test of success in faith lies in our actions. Faith that is not backed by the conviction of our deeds is a leaky boat for crossing the river of life. Sometimes we know our own faith only when presented with tests; then we must act on the courage of our beliefs. When we act in accordance with high ideals, we earn God's grace to progress further. Experience in spiritual endeavor confers knowledge; practice earns grace.

An individual who has faith in God must put his faith into practice. By believing in God and yet by ignoring God's utterances and commands, you are contradicting yourselves. Faith is not a cloak that is worn outside for deceiving others.

Summer Showers 1977, p. 218

Experience of the Lord's grace grants the certainty of self-realization. When the caterpillar of faith is transformed into the butterfly of knowledge, there is no further room for doubt. Once the nectar of divinity is tasted, there is no hunger for the bitter fruits of the world.

> *Do not waver or doubt when once you are convinced. Seek to understand and satisfy yourself. After that, do not be misled. When the sun is over your head, there will be no shadow; similarly, when faith is steady in your head, it should not cast any shadow of doubt.*
> *Sathya Sai Speaks 1, p. 25*

God can be known as surely as day follows night. Divine vision is more real than the experience of this transient world. Life changes constantly; God alone is unchanging. Only a life based on divine principles truly rests upon a solid foundation.

> *Faith in God is the secure foundation on which hope has to be built. The faith has to be stable and strong. The feeling that God will come to our rescue has to be vivid and vital, motivating and activating all that we do or speak or think.*
> *Sathya Sai Speaks 7, p. 232*

Faith grants us our true freedom. Holding fast to the divine will, we release our hold on fear and anxiety. God guides us through the maze of life. The Lord's voice is heard in the stillness of the heart; for his voice is our own voice; his strength is the strength of our faith and courage. Our own divine self, the God within, grants success.

> *Rely on the Lord within and discover inexhaustable reinforcements of courage within each heart. The final victory is for those who have faith in the invincible atma, their reality.*
> *Sathya Sai Speaks 5, p. 41*

7. Realization of the Goal

The saints and sages have trodden the razor-edged path to victory. By following their examples, we have little to lose and much to gain. Some petty pleasures are discarded, but the divine bliss that we gain is a far greater prize. Soon this short life will end and what will we have achieved? The material acquisitions will be left behind; the only treasure we will keep is the degree of evolution attained. All virtue earned lifts us closer to God-realization in this life or the next.

> *Whoever has the enthusiasm, the steadfastness, and the determination to reach the goal will certainly succeed. Cultivate that faith in ultimate success; never despair or fault or doubt. That is my advice to one and all.*
>
> *Sathya Sai Speaks 2, p. 141*

Questions for Study Circle

1. Why must faith come before experience?

2. Is faith in conflict with reason?

3. Is faith emotional?

4. Is faith an act of will?

5. Why do some people receive experiences that strengthen their faith, while others do not?

6. Is faith essential to know God?

7. What are the obstacles to faith?

8. How do we develop faith?

9. Is faith essential for a good life?

10. Is faith necessary for happiness?

11. Can faith move mountains?

References for Further Study

1. Sathya Sai Speaks 2, p. 22 (Hold on to faith).

2. Sathya Sai Speaks 2, pp. 98-102.

3. Sathya Sai Speaks 3, p. 224 (Radha's faith).

4. Sathya Sai Speaks 11, p. 107 (Do not put too much faith in worldly things).

5. Sathya Sai Speaks 11, pp. 107-108.

6. Summer Showers 1974, p. 290 (Faith in self is faith in God).

7. Summer Showers 1979, p. 42 (The benefit derived from faith is proportionate to its intensity).

8. Vidya Vahini, p. 9 (Spiritual benefit is tied to faith).

CHAPTER FIVE

Self-Confidence: The Basis for Faith in God

1. Prerequisite to Achievement

The early explorers, who left Europe to sail west in search of new lands, were filled with confidence. They had faith that they would not fall off the "edge" of the world. They were confident of their destination and of their ability to reach that destination. As a result, they discovered a new world of wonder and wealth.

Self-confidence is also an indispensable attribute of the successful spiritual explorer. Little, if anything, is accomplished without confidence in oneself. We must have confidence that we will accomplish the task, that we will travel the path to our destination. Without hope for a successful conclusion, there can be little enthusiasm for the journey. We must be convinced of our own innate divinity. There is no place for self-condemnation, which causes us to question our worthiness to succeed.

> *Without self-confidence, no achievement is possible. If you have confidence in your strength and skill, you can draw upon the inner springs of courage and raise yourselves to a higher level of joy and peace. For confidence in yourselves arises through the atma, which is your inner reality. The atma is peace, it is joy, it is strength, it is wisdom. So it is from the atma that you draw all these equipments for spiritual progress.*
>
> *Sathya Sai Speaks 6, p. 102*

Without self-confidence, we are tossed on the stormy seas of confusion and doubt. Without that deep faith in ourselves, we are driven from port to port, never finding the rest we seek. The fulfillment of our search in the world is found within ourselves. Whatever satisfaction we find around us is a reflection of our inner contentment.

> *The first thing you have to do is develop self-confidence. It is people who have no confidence in their own self who begin to wander about and to waver and to take to various different paths.*
>
> *Sathya Sai Speaks 9, p. 184*

Even material progress is based on faith in ourselves, in our own ability to accomplish a task. We achieve little if we are swayed by the criticisms of the crowd. We must chart a course and then hold to it, undisturbed by the inevitable ups and downs along the way. Like the early explorers, we may not find exactly what we expect, but we are sure to expand our horizons. We must value our own inner vision and our ability to manifest that vision in our lives.

> Don't deny the validity of your own experience. Stand on your strength, be unmoved either by adulation or denigration. Follow my lead: I am unaffected by either, I march on alone, undeterred and of my own accord. I am my own guide and witness; have full faith in this.
>
> *Sathya Sai Speaks 6, p. 107*

2. Faith in Self, Faith in God

An engineer who plans a tall building knows the importance of a strong foundation. To reach great heights, he must first dig down to a firm base in the earth. It would be foolish to build upon shifting sands, for the structure would soon topple. The firm foundation for faith in God is faith in self. When we reach down to the solid basis in ourselves, our progress is assured.

If we cannot find our own inner strength, how will we recognize divine power? Faith in self is the basis for faith in God, for it is the divinity within that enables us to recognize the divinity in the world. If we had never tasted the sweetness of sugar, why would we seek it out in the candy store?

> Self-confidence is the basis of faith in God also. People who do not know who they are and who have no confidence in their own strength and power assert that there is no God. But how can they declare that the God in whom you believe and who exists for you does not exist?
>
> *Sathya Sai Speaks 8, p. 88*

Divinity lies hidden within every person. Spiritual discipline reveals it. Like deriving butter from milk, certain methods are required to make divinity emerge. When we act on our aspirations with faith in our ability, we earn God's grace and guidance in the task. Those who make the effort, seizing every chance for advancement, earn that grace.

Everyone has the right to earn grace, but those like Ramakrishna, who have faith in themselves, will earn it soon and plentifully. God loves those who have the self-confidence and the courage of conviction and who seize every opportunity to improve their spiritual status.

Sathya Sai Speaks 7, p. 10

Self-confidence arises from the atma, the inner reality. Even if we do not recognize the source of our strength, it is enough if we heed its direction. The voice within is the unfailing guide to higher experience. It manifests as a thirst for truth and goodness. It assures us of our abilities and worth. It discloses the paths of right and wrong.

Your self is God. You have faith in your judgment, your intelligence, your ability, because God within tells you not to falter or fear. That assurance wells from within, from your basic truth, which is otherwise called God. It does not matter if you do not call it God. It is enough if you believe in yourself: that is the real test of theism.

Sathya Sai Speaks 2, p. 26

3. A Formula for Success

Great achievements grow from confidence and a plan. When Noah heard the voice of God, he set about to build an ark. He did not question his boat-building skills. He did not despair at his possible inability to make so many animals live together in a small boat. He had confidence in his own ability to learn all the necessary skills for the project. The town folk who came to jeer could not deter Noah from his plan. He maintained his self-confidence and acted on the Lord's command.

Little is accomplished without formulating a plan and adhering to it. To manifest the divine vision, we must have faith in the goal and in God. We may not always choose the quickest path, but we learn along the way. No progress is made without some mistakes. Obstacles help us develop strength and stamina. With time and experience, we reach the goal.

Have faith in yourself, your own capacity to adhere to a strict timetable of sadhana (spiritual discipline), your own ability to reach the goal of realization. When you have no faith in the wave, how can you get faith in the ocean?

Sathya Sai Speaks 5, p. 230

When we have confidence in our own abilities and faith in God, we can accomplish any task. Faith in self and faith in God grant the strength and patience to achieve any victory.

Devotion and self-confidence are like the negative and positive. It is the combination of these two that will enable us to fulfill our sacred thought.

Summer Showers 1977, p. 97

4. Self-Realization

Self-realization is the ultimate stage of self-confidence. It is the conclusion of self-development. When we attain that blissful state, we will know that all beauty, all joy, and all peace lie within us. The answers to all questions are within, for we are ourselves the answer. In the light of our expanded awareness, we will see that we are indeed God.

To achieve the blissful state of divine vision we must cultivate true self-satisfaction. Satisfaction is contentment. It eliminates desire and allows us to see the unity of creation. When we grasp the vision of unity, we are able to sacrifice the small ego-self that limits our loyalty and sympathy. Then we can assume our true identity as God -- the life-force behind all we see.

You should develop self-confidence, and with that you will get self-satisfaction. Once you acquire self-satisfaction, you will be able to show self-sacrifice, and this will result in self-realization. Self-realization thus ultimately depends on the base of self-confidence.

Summer Showers 1973, p. 249

Questions for Study Circle

1. Where does self-confidence originate?
2. Of what use is self-confidence?
3. How is self-confidence manifested in daily life?
4. How is self-confidence cultivated?
5. How is self-confidence related to self-realization?
6. Can we have confidence in God without confidence in self?
7. Is spiritual progress possible without self-confidence?

8. What are the obstacles to confidence in self?

9. Can we have too much self-confidence?

References for Further Study

1. Sathya Sai Speaks 9, p. 186 (Self-realization is derived from self-confidence).

2. Sathya Sai Speaks 10, p. 90 (The self-confidence of Hanuman).

3. Summer Showers 1972, p. 117 (Self-confidence is required for the spiritual journey).

4. Summer Showers 1977, p. 97 (Self-confidence of Hanuman).

5. Vidya Vahini, pp. 81-82.

CHAPTER SIX

Discipline: Means to an End

1. What is Discipline?

The root of the word **discipline** comes from the Latin word for instruction. Spiritual disciplines are means of self-instruction that we engage in for the growth of our higher awareness. The successful practice of self-transformation requires a high degree of inner discipline. We must learn the lessons and practice the rules of the spiritual path to achieve success.

Discipline is inherent in both nature and humanity. The planets conform to their orbits, and each creature acts according to its character. Physical laws of discipline govern such things as the crystalline structure of rocks. Everything from the largest to the smallest in creation adheres to its own law. It is only in the working of the laws of nature that each being finds its proper place in the cosmos. For humanity, the highest disciplines are the transpersonal. Such disciplines enable us to realize our identity with God.

What are the necessary disciplines for us to practice? We must obey the rule of law in society and the rule of the heart in our personal conduct. Through education and experience, we learn the laws of the land. Through self-inquiry, we understand the rule of spirit. Unthinking habit is not discipline. Discipline is a reasoned course of practice for the production of specific results. Sathya Sai Baba recommends certain disciplines for our spiritual unfoldment. These disciplines include:

1. Do not harm others (ahimsa).

2. Speak the truth and practice what you teach (sathya).

3. Study the teachings of the scriptures and the saints.

4. Serve others without seeking reward.

5. Practice devotion to God.

6. Practice detachment from objects of desire.

7. Do your duty to yourself, family, community, and nation.

8. Live within the bounds of morality.

9. Meditate on the unity of creation and the omnipresence of God.

These are some of the practices by which we shed our ignorance and enter the light of self-knowledge.

2. Benefits of Right Action

We have great freedom to determine our own path of action. We carry within ourselves the seeds of either self-destruction or self-realization. We can ignore the call of our divine nature and remain mired in the material world, or we can listen to the call and realize the highest attainments. If we learn from the world around us and chart a disciplined course of action, we can earn our true freedom. When we rush to satisfy material desires, we suffer the consequences.

> *The lesson is learned by man when he studies nature, analyzing it and trying to understand it...Break the laws of nature and she boxes you in the ear; obey her commands and listen to her warnings and she will pass on to you your heritage of immortality.*
>
> *Sathya Sai Speaks 2, p. 152*

When we aspire to reach a great height, we must first build a strong foundation. A groundwork must be prepared before the structure rises. Proper preparations must be made to insure success. This is true in all fields: in the trades, in business, in the arts. It is of paramount importance in the spiritual field.

> *Discipline is essential for the success of every endeavor of man, whatever the field, whether it be economic, social, educational, or merely material and worldly. It is even more essential for success in spiritual effort.*
>
> *Sathya Sai Speaks 7, p. 328*

External disciplines, such as the law of the land or the physical laws of cause and effect, are fairly easy to understand. They usually result in quick, adverse consequences for those who overstep their bounds. Self-discipline is more difficult to comprehend: the relationship between inner causes and effects is less apparent. However, the disciplines which we impose on ourselves are just as important to our welfare. The consequences of right discipline are just as certain as the results of physical laws. A spiritual program must be carefully considered and then skillfully followed if we are to reach self-fulfillment.

The real you is the atma. This can be learned only by constant meditation, by moving in good company, by listening to the talks of realized men, by following some prescribed course of discipline. That is why I lay so much emphasis on discipline.

Sathya Sai Speaks 4, p. 159

3. Our True Freedom

Discipline is usually considered to be restricting. Actually, quite the opposite is true. In material life, as in spiritual life, we gain our freedom only through discipline. Hard work endows us with material rewards such as a home or automobile. In spiritual life, we win freedoms of greater worth. We win the freedom of a joyful and peaceful life. Above all, we win God's grace, which alleviates our suffering and grants us the opportunity to continue to advance on our Godward way.

In spiritual matters, the more we subject ourselves to discipline, the more joy and peace we are able to enjoy.

Sathya Sai Speaks 4, p. 306

Although disciplines seem restrictive at first, with time we recognize them as the source of our joy. Self-discipline gives birth to confidence and satisfaction. An individual without self-discipline finds no lasting happiness. As a world with no laws would disintegrate into chaos, an individual without self-discipline becomes mired in confusion and despair. Understanding and adhering to the rules of the game grant us joy.

In fact, it is the rules and the restrictions that give charm to the game of life. In the game of football, if any player can do anything with the ball and there is neither foul nor out, neither offside nor goal, neither throw nor penalty, then it will be a meaningless game incapable of giving ananda (joy).

Sathya Sai Speaks 2, p. 219

4. Key to a Productive Life

Even material freedoms yield little satisfaction if we are held captive by the demons of fear, anger, and worry. Without the benefit of spiritual discipline, material discipline is shallow consolation. The quest for true freedom is won by disciplined study and action. When we digest the messages of the saints and sages who have already trodden the path, we can assimilate their wisdom and experience.

The sages have discovered the disciplines that will keep you unaffected by defeat or victory, loss or gain. Learn them, practice them. Establish yourself in unruffled peace.

Sathya Sai Speaks 6, p. 226

Other sources of wisdom, such as the holy texts of the world's major living religions, may also provide the traditional knowledge necessary to adopt a course of spiritual discipline.

So man has to be to be guided by the wisdom of the past, the bounds prescribed by his well-wishers, the sages, the sastras (holy texts) or moral codes laid down to map the conscience in him.

Sathya Sai Speaks 6, p. 109

As seekers of wisdom, we hold the keys of knowledge in our hearts. The promptings of the conscience show us the disciplines to follow. But we must act on our knowledge for it to yield results. Although we may possess ample devotion and wisdom, if we are not employed in a disciplined course of action, there will be no benefit.

You may have devotion, you may discharge the duty entrusted to you, but unless you are saturated in discipline, the other two are useless.

Sathya Sai Speaks 9, p. 14

5. Maintain Discipline

Self-discipline can be difficult to maintain. Particularly at the start of the spiritual path, the obstacles seem formidable. The need for many changes in our lifestyles and attitudes becomes quickly apparent. It is easy for the beginner to become discouraged. There is also a danger of the student becoming compulsive about discipline and laying too much emphasis on the self. It is best for us to progress slowly and carefully at the outset. Discipline must be cultivated early in life and practiced consistently. Then when hardships arise, they can be overcome with the help of our inner strength.

Discipline comes to the rescue during crisis when the world flows toward you as a dark flood of hate or derision, or when those in whom you have put your trust shun contact and shy away. Without discipline, the mind of man is turned into a wild elephant in a rut. You have to catch it young and train it so that its strength and skill can be useful to man and harmless to life around.

Sathya Sai Speaks 7, p. 418

With proper preparation, we learn to overcome obstacles. As self-discipline increases, the task becomes easier. However, repeated attempts must still be made to achieve success. Very rarely do we make progress without repeated attempts to master a difficulty. A systematic and controlled disciplinary plan is the foremost weapon in the battle.

It is chiefly a matter of careful, well-timed, regulated discipline. It cannot be obtained by spurts and skips, but must be climbed step by step, each step being used as a foothold for the next...You have to learn each lesson by systematic study. Application and effort alone will give success.

Sathya Sai Speaks 1, p. 166

Fortitude and persistence assure realization of the goal. Each obstacle is a test. We may only pass on to the next higher level when we have mastered the first. We should look forward to tests as chances to prove our progress in spiritual discipline. Each obstacle can be mastered one at a time. The wise person will not put off the opportunity to surmount a barrier. Each day lost in the prime of life yields one less day at the end of life to achieve self-realization. Therefore, discipline must not be relinquished before realization is attained.

You should never give up the habit of discipline. When you reach the state of perfection only, you do not have to think of regulations or discipline.

Summer Showers 1972, p. 282

6. Duties of a Devotee

Discipline is particularly important for those who consider themselves to be devotees of Sathya Sai Baba. Devotees of Sai Baba must exemplify what they have learned. As Sai Baba's life is his message, so the devotee also attempts to act as an example. It is by the example of the devotees that the master is known.

People, those outwardly "distant" from Swami, he tells, but not so severely as those "near." People judge Swami by his "near" devotees and so these individuals must follow very strict standards of behavior.

Conversations, p. 111

Aspirants who make a greater commitment are required to assume more discipline. The greater the growth we wish to realize, the more self-discipline we must exercise to fulfill our responsibility. But it should not be thought a burden. It is an opportunity for our own benefit.

Generally, I speak sweet, but on this matter of discipline, I will not grant any concessions...I will insist on strict obedience. I shall not reduce the rigor to suit your level, for that will only ruin you. I pay attention to your ultimate good.

Sathya Sai Speaks 2, p. 186

7. Chart a Course

If we heed the call of regular practice and persist in our quest, then we will surely attain the goal. Perseverence and intensity pay the dividend of self-realization. God is in all, but to find him we must follow a course of spiritual discipline. Divinity appears to those who complete the necessary practices.

But the question is asked, "Then why is he (God) not seen?" Well, he is as butter is in milk, in every drop, through and through. If butter is to be seen, then certain processes have to be done -- boiling, curdling, churning, etc. So, too, by certain spiritual disciplines like repeating the name on the tongue, he who dwells in the heart can be visualized; the immanent God can be experienced as real.

Sathya Sai Speaks 7, p. 362

When victory is achieved, the rules and regulations may be transcended. When that blissful day arrives, the realized individual overcomes the dogmas and tools of the path. That joyful state confers the ultimate freedom of God-realization in which all is recognized as divine.

It is good to be born in a church, but it is not good to die in it. Grow and rescue yourselves from the limits and regulations, the doctrines that fence your freedom of thought, the ceremonial rites that restrict and redirect. Reach the point where churches do not matter, where all roads end, from where all roads run.

Sathya Sai Speaks 7, p. 82-83

Questions for Study Circle

1. What is discipline?

2. How much discipline is enough?

3. Is it more difficult to live with discipline or without it?

4. Can there be too much discipline?

5. What is the best kind of discipline?

6. Who has the right to discipline another?

7. How do we discipline ourselves?

8. How do we know if we have enough discipline?

9. Does discipline restrict freedom?

10. Is there a time when self-discipline becomes unnecessary?

11. What spiritual disciplines should we undertake?

12. What are the immediate spiritual rewards of self-discipline?

References for Further Study

1. Dhyana Vahini, p. 2.

2. Sathya Sai Speaks 5, p. 7 (Discipline helps us discover the basis of creation).

3. Sathya Sai Speaks 5, p. 185 (Discipline must be started early).

4. Sathya Sai Speaks 7, p. 328.

5. Sathya Sai Speaks 8, pp. 24, 66-67.

6. Summer Showers 1978, p. 201 (Discipline should be constant).

7. Summer Roses on the Blue Mountains, p. 46.

CHAPTER SEVEN

Dharma and Duty:

The Right Action at the Right Time

1. Dharma: What Is It?

In Hindu tradition, dharma is generally interpreted as spiritual duty. But dharma is more than that: it is a sense of religious obligation that combines concepts of both duty and reason. There is no equivalent English word. Dharma entails responsibility to self, others, and God. It is not a set of restrictive laws; it is the liberating concept of doing the right thing at the right time. It is based on a reasoned course of action performed out of wise love. Dharma requires introspection and self-discipline based on the knowledge of inner divinity. It results in a joyful and contented life.

> The word dharma does not mean duty: in duty there is no freedom. In reason there is freedom, and in religious obligation there is the union between duty and reason. Dharma, then, refers to religious obligation, and in that word are the concepts of both duty and reason.
>
> *Conversations, p. 15*

2. How Do We Perform Our Dharma?

How is dharma, or spiritual obligation, expressed in action? The specifics depend on time and circumstance. However, some general precepts apply at all times. Dharma requires adherence to truth, nonviolence, and universal love.

> And what is dharma? Practicing what you preach, doing as you say it has to be done, keeping precept and practice in line. Earn virtuously, yearn piously; live in the fear of God, live for reaching God: that is dharma.
>
> *Sathya Sai Speaks 4, p. 339*

When consciously starting the spiritual life, we need to remember the basics. The basic truths are known to all; they are the lessons taught by the religions of all lands. These lessons are summarized in the Golden Rule: "Do unto others as you would have them do unto you." They teach consideration for others and respect for our own divinity.

> *What exactly is your duty? Let me summarize it for you. First, tend your parents with love and reverence and gratitude. Second, speak the truth and act virtuously. Third, whenever you have a few moments to spare, repeat the name of the Lord with the form in your mind. Fourth, never indulge in talking ill of others or try to discover faults in others. And finally, do not cause pain to others in any form.*
> *Sathya Sai Speaks 4, pp. 348-349*

The rules of dharma may be further summarized as the path of virtue. All people know generally what is right and what is wrong. If they do not act on that knowledge, they deny their spiritual obligation.

> *Dharma is characterized by holiness, peace, truth, and fortitude. Dharma is yoga, union, merger; it is sathya (truth). Its attributes are justice, sense control, sense of honor, love, dignity, goodness, meditation, sympathy, nonviolence: such is dharma that persists through the ages. It leads one on to universal love and unity.*
> *Dharma Vahini, p. 21*

3. A Role for Everyone

Our duties depend on our karmic inheritance, age, and position in life. We have duties in the world and duties in spiritual practice. Some duties are to ourselves; some are to others. For example, it may be appropriate for young people to work and establish a place for themselves in the world. It is not wrong to earn a living and possibly gain wealth if we earn honestly and use wealth for the benefit of others. In youth we have family and social responsibilities. However, when we reach an advanced age we have the duty of detaching from the world and fulfilling our spiritual search. Some of our duties are based on age; others relate to gender or position in life.

So, too, every profession, every stage of life, each sex, each period of life as fixed by age -- childhood, boyhood, adolescence, youth, middle age, old age -- has duties and obligations, which set the norm and guide the individual to benefit himself and society.

Sathya Sai Speaks 6, p. 120

Each of us must follow his or her own path. It is better to do our own duty poorly than to perform another's duty well. The duties we are called to perform may be determined by circumstances or factors beyond our control. Our freedom to follow a chosen course may be limited due to our obligations. One individual may have freedom to choose his or her own path, while another may be restricted to a narrow range of opportunities. Each of us has personal duties and opportunities resulting from our past actions. We may exercise limited choice in determining what our program will be.

Dharma is like a mother. One can choose a wife, but no one can choose a mother. Dharma is in the same position as one's mother is. We have no choice and we cannot transform dharma.

Summer Showers 1974, p. 293

4. Like What You Have to Do

True happiness in life results from performing our duty well. It is not derived from enjoying temporary pleasures. Hard work, done to fulfill our obligations, yields the greatest satisfaction. The pursuit of sensuous pleasures ends in eventual regrets.

The secret of happiness is not in doing what one likes, but in liking what one has to do. Whatever work you have to do, you should do it with pleasure and liking.

Summer Showers 1977, p. 100

5. Your Heart Will Be Your Guide

The way to determine our unique duty is to listen to the voice within. No one else can tell us what our duty is. Our conscience alone is the true guide in all situations. When we accept its guidance, it leads us to a joyful and contented life.

Your conscience knows the real source of joy; it will prod you towards the right path. Your business is to take it as a "guide" and not disobey it every time it contradicts your fancy.

Sathya Sai Speaks 1, p. 91

The voice within directs us to our spiritual destination. That inner guidance is the voice of God. When we follow its direction, we draw closer to God. It helps us to be mindful of our dharma. When we are aware of it each moment, we become more attuned to our spiritual obligation. With practice the conscience can quickly evaluate any situation and point the path to joy and peace.

The body is the temple of God. In every body, God is installed, whether the owner of the body recognizes it or not. It is God that inspires you to good acts and warns you against the bad. Listen to that voice. Obey that voice and you will not come to any harm.

Sathya Sai Speaks 2, p. 26

When we overcome the negative pulls of egoism and vice, we find ourselves naturally drawn to the dharmic path. When the clouds of anger and hate recede, the sun of love shines forth. That sunshine is our natural state. It appears automatically when the dark clouds of ego are dispersed. Then we recognize God within ourselves and others. It enables us to love and serve others, relinquishing greed and attachment to fleeting objects.

Whoever subdues his egoism, conquers his selfish desires, destroys his bestial feelings and impulses, and gives up the natural tendency to regard the body as self, he is surely on the path of dharma. He knows that the goal of dharma is the merging of the wave in the sea, the merging of the self in the Overself.

Dharma Vahini, p. 4

The performance of our obligation should be an act of love, not a duty done begrudgingly. It is our recognition of our place in God's creation. To serve with a grudge or without enthusiasm indicates our own lack of vision, for God is in all people, and service to others is service to God. Love is the true characteristic of humanity.

Duty without love is deplorable.

Duty with love is desirable.

Love without duty is divine.

Summer Showers 1979, p. 160

The journey of self-transformation is long and difficult. Many obstacles lie on the path. Even family and friends may try to deter us from the quest. To succeed we must listen to our hearts and not be discouraged by criticism or the unfounded concerns of others.

> *When you travel towards God, whoever objects has to be bypassed. Prahlada went against his father, Vibhisana went against his brother, Jamadagni had to harm his own mother, Meera could not obey her husband: they stuck to the path of God and broke through all those who opposed them.*
>
> *Sathya Sai Speaks 7, p. 444*

6. Service: Responsibility to Society

Service is a sacred duty to society. It is an integral aspect of spiritual life. Performing service discharges our debt to society, which has provided us with food, shelter, security, and other blessings. It purifies our hearts and minds, making us fit to realize our inner divinity. At times correct action can even stimulate correct belief. The inner satisfaction of service gives us joy and the will to do more. Sathya Sai Baba does not counsel devotees to live as hermits. He teaches us to work in the world for the betterment of society. Engaging in the task of uplifting humanity is a duty and a form of worship.

> *If God himself is here to foster dharma and you engage yourself in the same task, then you are worshipping him. Then you are near and dear to him, for you are serving him, his devotees, and yourself.*
>
> *Conversations, p. 41*

Whatever our duty, it should be performed with dedication. Raising a family or working at a seemingly "unspiritual" job are actually services to God. Each of us must learn the lessons appropriate to our needs. The Lord gives us tasks in life that enable us to reach spiritual fulfillment. No task is too small or unimportant to do well.

Whatever you do, wherever you are placed, believe that God has put you there for that work.

Sathya Sai Speaks 9, p. 20

The Lord does not separate tasks into categories of his work and other work. He is everywhere and is worshipped in the performance of all duties. It is not possible to separate the temporal from the spiritual. We cannot do spiritual work while neglecting family and social responsibilities.

Veda (the sacred teaching) has told us that it is a sin to divide our work into two parts and to say that something is your work and something is God's work. In all the work that we have to do in our life, there is nothing that you can call your own work. Everything is God's work. You should do all your work believing that it is God's work and then the omnipresent Lord will take care of the results.

Summer Showers 1974, p. 216

7. Remember the Director of the Play

God's grace is earned even in common tasks, if they are dedicated to him. Village ladies balance pots of water on their heads in rural Indian towns. They may chat with neighbors or watch their children, but always their mind is on the pot of water balanced above. We also must perform action in the world while remaining concentrated on our duty -- remembrance of God.

A little practice will teach you to hold fast to the feet of God while roaming about in the world, doing all duties and carrying all responsibilities as dedicated to him.

Sathya Sai Speaks 5, p. 276

The results of our actions are less important than the manner in which we perform them. We must work to the best of our ability; the results are decided by God. It is our duty to perform action dedicated to the highest ideals, but it is foolish for us to be too concerned with the results. If we act on good motivation and follow our hearts, the results will take care of themselves.

*Do all work as actors in a play, keeping your identity
separate and not attached to your personality or your role.
Remember that the whole thing is just a play and the Lord
has assigned you a part. Act well your part: there all your
duty ends. He has designed the play and he enjoys it.*

Teachings, p. 109

Learning our duty is like the unfolding of a flower. The flower exists
within the bud, but is only seen as it blossoms. All of us have the
fragrance of love in our hearts, but we must act unselfishly to release it.
Truth and divinity are always present within us; it is their manifestation
that is often lacking in our lives. So also the avatar incarnates not to
reestablish dharma, but to make it apparent.

*It is not dharma which needs to be reestablished, for dharma
is unchanging and indestructible. It is the practice of dharma
for which the avatars are born.*

Summer Roses on the Blue Mountains, p. 21

8. Duty to the Divine Self

Each of us has within the potential for realizing our divinity. Divinity
manifests when we listen to the voice in our hearts and act according to
our duty. With time and practice, each of us is rewarded with joy and
peace. The performance of duty earns for us the opportunity to perform
more responsible duties. When the inner voice is heeded, we expand
into unbounded freedom.

*To be free is your birthright, not to be bound. It is only when
you guide your steps along the path illumined by the
universal unbound dharma that you are really free...*

Dharma Vahini, p. 10

As we approach the latter stages of life, the cultivation of detachment
and wisdom acquire primary importance. Our highest duty is to realize
our divinity. Our unique characteristic as human beings is our ability
for introspection, which we have been given for this purpose. The birds
and animals share many other functions, but we alone have the capacity
and duty to discover the residence of God within.

Your duty is to yearn for the attainment of the consciousness of the One, behind all this apparent multiplicity.

Sathya Sai Speaks 7, p. 507

Questions for Study Circle

1. What is dharma?

2. Is duty the same as work?

3. Are duty and dharma the same?

4. Do we have a predetermined dharma in life?

5. Is spiritual obligation the same for everyone?

6. Who or what determines our dharma?

7. Does dharma always remain the same?

8. What duties do we owe to others?

9. What duties do we owe ourselves?

10. What is the relationship between dharma and conscience?

11. Are some duties spiritual and other duties worldly?

References for Further Study

1. Conversations, p. 140 (The Golden Rule is the test of dharma).

2. Dharma Vahini (Entire book).

3. Gita Vahini, pp. 56-59.

4. Sathya Sai Speaks 2, pp. 219-220.

5. Sathya Sai Speaks 4, p. 109 (Each must determine his own dharma).

6. Sathya Sai Speaks 6, p. 257 (The Lord is most pleased by dharma).

7. Sathya Sai Speaks 6, p. 307 (Dharma is the inner voice of God, shaped by history and asceticism).

8. Sathya Sai Speaks 7, p. 498 (Man's duty is psychological transformation).

9. Sathya Sai Speaks 9, pp. 87-88 (Pandavas' adherence to duty).

10. Summer Showers 1972, pp. 115-116 (Do not swerve from your duty).

11. Summer Showers 1973, p. 200 (Dharma reveals oneness).

12. Summer Showers 1973, p. 207 (Dharma protects those who protect dharma).

13. Summer Showers 1973, p. 208 (Dharma is following the Golden Rule).

14. Summer Showers 1979, pp. 6-8.

15. Summer Showers 1979, pp. 25-26 (Individual dharma-swadharma).

16. Summer Showers 1979, p. 171-172.

17. Summer Roses on the Blue Mountains, p. 48 (Dharma protects those who protect dharma).

18. Truth, What is Truth? Vol. 1, p. 88.

19. Vidya Vahini, p. 4 (Test of dharma: does it promote detachment or greed?).

CHAPTER EIGHT

Morality: Foundation for Progress

1. Religion Is Three-Fourths Character

Morality is the foundation for spiritual progress. It is the prerequisite for the journey, the first step. If we do not live a moral life, our pursuit of advanced practices is meaningless. Yet today many people desire quick character changes and miraculous results before developing even basic virtues. Righteousness and character are the essential qualifications for the journey.

> *Religion is three-fourths character. No person can claim to be religious if he merely observes the sacraments and rules, and fails to be upright and compassionate.*
>
> *Sathya Sai Speaks 7, p. 153*

Virtuous character is the driving force of every dedicated aspirant. However knowledgeable, devoted, or active we may be, if we lack virtue we are destined to fail. Moral strength reflects our practice of universal values and endows us with a willingness to act on what we have learned. It demonstrates a personality that integrates the various facets of our discipline. Only a strongly integrated personality is capable of great achievement.

> *It is often declared that knowledge is power. No. No. Character is power. Nothing can be more powerful on Earth than character. Riches, scholarship, status, authority are all frail and flimsy before it.*
>
> *Sathya Sai Speaks 11, p. 235*

Today many teachers present courses for "quick" spiritual development that do not address this essential first step. They prescribe breathing exercises, postures, or special meditations for new students without imposing any preliminary qualifications of virtuous character. But advanced practices cannot yield realization of our divine nature without adherence to basic standards of right conduct.

You may do the most rigorous japa (repetition of the name of the Lord) or submit yourself to the direst of austerities, but if you are not virtuous, all of it is sheer waste.

Sathya Sai Speaks 4, p. 218

It is impossible for aspirants to seek their advanced degrees without first learning the alphabet of virtue. Higher degrees may be obtained only after first learning the basics. Living a moral life is the essential first step in reducing egoism. If we do not conquer selfish desires, there is no hope for us to expand beyond the small perimeter of ourselves. The modern cults of body and personality cater to the lower self. This trend needs to be reversed. Consideration of and service to others is required on the spiritual path.

Morality, a virtuous character: these are the very foundations of progress, the very basic needs. They grow in the realm of the spirit. But, today, the spirit is neglected. Physical and animal needs are catered to. They are accepted as the ends of living; all efforts are directed to these.

Sathya Sai Speaks 7, p. 336

2. What Is Morality?

But what is morality? It is adherence to truth, love, goodness, duty, peace, and nonviolence -- to God's will as we understand it. These are the human values that are the core teachings of the world's religions. Maintaining high moral standards demonstrates our recognition of the divinity in others and in ourselves. It shows our respect and consideration for others in thought and deed. Morality is more than simply obeying certain laws or social norms. It is the observance of these high qualities which makes us truly human and potentially self-realized.

Morality is the corollary to dharma (spiritual duty). Morality does not merely mean the observance of certain rules in the workaday world. Morality means adherence to the straight and sacred path of right conduct. Morality is the blossoming of good conduct.

Sanathana Sarathi, Jan. 1985, p. 2

Morality, like dharma, is suited to our particular role in society. It is based on our age, sex, status, and function. There are no absolute laws of morality. The norms of morality vary from age to age and from culture to culture. Ernest Hemingway observed in *Death in the Afternoon:* "...What is moral is what you feel good after and what is immoral is what you feel bad after..."

> *There are no universal and absolute norms of morality. Ethical relativity is an inescapable social phenomenon. Morality depends on the time, the place, and the spirit of the age.*
>
> *Summer Showers 1979, p. 25*

3. How Can We Become Virtuous?

In the beginning the lessons are plain: do not lie, do not cheat, do not steal, do no harm to others. The consequences of such misguided actions are quickly realized. Yet, despite the fact that suffering inevitably follows selfish action, some people take little precaution to avoid it. Although we may be burned repeatedly, some of us continue to reach into the fire.

> *The saddest part of the story is that man, though he sees and hears, suffers and falls, does not get quite convinced that sin is a dangerous experiment, that it unmistakably brings on its harvest of tears.*
>
> *Sathya Sai Speaks 2, pp. 160-161*

When incorrect action is recognized as the source of pain, the battle is half won. The seeds of suffering can be pulled from the Earth before they sprout. With time, virtues rise to the fore. Serve others; love others as yourself; see divinity in all God's creatures. Through adherence to high moral standards, the grace of God may be won. Each step becomes easier and each good deed leads to another. When we follow the straight path of spiritual duty, God makes our load lighter and easier to bear. With each passing day our way becomes clearer. We learn that a virtuous character is our only lasting possession.

Be moral, be virtuous. Be sincere in thought, deed, and word. Be honest to yourself. Money comes and goes! But morality comes and grows! So man has to give up the yearning for money and yearn for more and more morality.
                                        Sathya Sai Speaks 7, p. 331

The drive to live virtuously is the essence of spirituality. It reflects our ability to distinguish the transitory from the real. Few people give much thought to the nearness of death, yet it may arrive at any moment. Death takes all our worldly possessions, however guarded and fostered they may have been. We are left only with our qualities of being. The value of our lives will be appraised not by the accumulation of our possessions, but by our discernment of spiritual reality -- and our willingness to act on that vision.

Do not think that only those who worship a picture or image with pompous paraphernalia are devotees. Whoever walks straight along the moral path, whoever acts as he speaks and speaks as he has seen, whoever melts at another's woe and exults at another's joy...is a devotee, perhaps a greater devotee.
                                        Sathya Sai Speaks 2, pp. 22-23

We do not require another person to show us right conduct. Right conduct is a function of our conscience, the voice within. The pursuit of a moral life is an unfolding journey, which takes us toward the God within. It is the heart of spiritual practice, which carries us from the most basic lessons on the path to realization of formless divinity. That search is our true reason for living. We fulfill our duty when we value virtue rather than material possessions.

Moral and spiritual values have to be honored as much as, if not more than, economic and material values. Life must be a harmonious blend of these values with emphasis on moral strength.
                                        Sathya Sai Speaks 8, p. 179

The integrity of a nation depends on the character of its citizens. A nation without moral standards follows the road of decline. If a nation is to make enduring contributions to the world, it must be founded on eternal values. A society, like an individual, earns God's grace based on its adherence to virtue.

The honor of a nation depends upon the morality of that nation. A nation without morality will be doomed.

Summer Showers 1972, p. 218

4. Love: The Basis of Morality

The means to cultivate moral strength is selfless love. When we recognize that the same divinity resides in others as resides in ourselves, we refrain from selfish action. By expanding our vision to encompass all within the atma, we are unable to hurt others. Love is the basis for the preservation and growth of society.

Morality has to be grown in the heart by feeding it with love; then only can we have justice, security, law, and order. If love declines among the people, nations will weaken and mankind will perish.

Sathya Sai Speaks 8, pp. 80-81

Questions for Study Circle

1. What is morality?

2. Who determines what is moral?

3. Are there certain specific rules of morality?

4. Does morality vary by culture or country?

5. How do we know when we have done something wrong?

6. Why do so many people dislike the word 'morality'?

7. Is Sai Baba's definition of morality the same as the meaning commonly used?

8. Can we progress spiritually without advancing morally?

References for Further Study

1. Gita Vahini, pp. 217-225 (The 20 virtues essential for jnana).

2. Gita Vahini, p. 298

3. Sathya Sai Speaks 5, p. 336 (Morality should be taught in conjunction with other subjects, not separately).

4. Sathya Sai Speaks 7, p. 404 (One evil deed will lead to another).

5. Summer Showers 1973, p. 164 (Even devotion is not protection from illusion if one does not have morality).

6. Summer Showers 1979, p. 24 (The respect commanded by a community depends on its moral strength).

CHAPTER NINE

Satsang: Company of the Holy

1. Why Seek Spiritual Company?

Men and women of great spiritual attainment are almost always found in the company of devotees and spiritual aspirants. Seekers are drawn to the light of such great beings, just as inspired teachers feel compelled to share their light, love, and wisdom with a world hungry for their gifts.

Good company lifts and carries us on the tide of spirituality. Unwholesome company washes us away on the dark current of self-indulgence and grief. Good fellowship provides us with regular sustenance and encouragement. Beneficial companionship aids our steady and lasting progress, which inspires us on the Godward path. Spiritual association encourages faith and grants us the strength to continue our quest -- even when the task seems most difficult. Keeping the company of holy-minded men and women can make the difference between success and failure in spiritual endeavor.

> *The easiest and most fruitful method of keeping yourself free from dust and rust is satsang (good company). The company of the good and the godly will slowly and surely chasten and cleanse the persons prone to straying away from the straight path towards self-realization.*
>
> *Sathya Sai Speaks 9, p. 223*

2. What Is Good Company?

Real friends encourage only the best in us. A true companion gives to others without seeking return. As a tree is known by its fruits, friends are known by their actions. Good company is association with those who seek to learn and practice truthfulness, love, duty, devotion, and peace. Such company encourages us to make our best effort on the divine path. Men and women who practice spiritual discipline are examples to each other and to the world. It is their nature to serve all, even those who seek to harm them.

> *When a sharp ax is used to cut a sandalwood tree, the sandalwood tree does not feel hurt by the ax, nor does it get angry with it. On the contrary, the sandalwood tree hands its fragrance to the ax...This is the quality of good people.*
>
>   *Summer Showers 1973, p. 53*

3. We Adapt to Our Surroundings

In nature all creatures adapt to their environments. The chameleon changes color to suit its habitat. The giraffe has developed a long neck to reach his meal of leaves on high tree branches. People also accommodate themselves to their surroundings. They develop tastes for available foods and they normally build their homes from materials obtainable locally.

A similar type of adaptation occurs in our minds. We naturally tend to agree with the attitudes and behaviors of those whose company we keep. We seek acceptance and approval from our peers. For this reason we must be certain to seek only good companionship. Particularly when we are new on the spiritual path, good company is indispensable. When the mind is not confirmed in the ways of good behavior and morality, it is easily led astray. Only great beings can change the world around them. The tendency of untrained minds is to adapt to their environments, at the expense of their spiritual aspirations.

> *There were two parrots on a tree, twins, to be more precise. A hunter trapped them and sold them, one to a low, cruel butcher and the other to a sage who was running an ashrama (school) to teach the Vedas (holy scriptures). After a few years, he was surprised to find that one bird swore very foully, while the other recited the leelas (divine play) of the Lord in a sweet musical tone which captivated the listeners. Such is the effect of the environment; so seek and secure satsang."*
>
>   *Sathya Sai Speaks 1, pp. 91-92*

Long practice and discipline are required to make the mind obey the divinity within. It is difficult to wean the mind from low desires. But by associating with high-minded friends, we can adopt aspirations and ideals similar to theirs. Beneficial company may be compared to sweet milk, while the company of bad people is like water. When a drop of milk is added to a pitcher of water, the milk loses its value. But when a small amount of water is added to a pitcher of milk, the water takes on the value of milk. As Rama is said to have admonished Lakshmana:

> *The company of bad men is the prelude to the disappearance of wisdom. The company of good men makes wisdom blossom.*
>
> *Ram Katha Rasavahini, p. 367*

4. Satsang, a Spiritual Discipline

Can we call the practice of choosing our company a spiritual discipline? The methods that help us to evolve spiritually are designed to purify our hearts and minds. Meditation, service, study -- all spiritual training has this aim as its purpose. Similarly, the company we keep directly influences our purity of mind.

The discipline of attending regular gatherings of aspirants, such as study circles or devotional meetings, is a great aid on the spiritual journey. We better understand the practical aspects of spirituality when we see them practiced by others. As we learn by observing Sai Baba's actions, we also learn by observing the lives of our peers. Practical demonstration is necessary for our education, as well as our own study and devotion.

> *Ascetic practices, years of constant recitation of the name, pilgrimages to holy places and shrines, study of sacred books -- these will not help the aspirant to spiritual victory as much as communion with the godly and good.*
>
> *Sathya Sai Speaks 6, p. 193*

The best way to combat wrong tendencies is to keep them out of sight and out of mind. The untrained mind seeks out inferior sights and sounds. To deter the mind from attaching itself to unwholesome influences, we must keep such influences far away. The recommended way to learn virtue is to keep it always in sight. High ideals inspire us to noble action. Mahatma Gandhi was inspired to live a life of truth after he witnessed a holy play about the life of the avatar Rama.

You are molded by the company you relish. When you make friends with the blacksmith, you are bound to collect black dust on your clothes and skin. That is why sangam, association, is held to be so crucial in spiritual life.

Sathya Sai Speaks 5, p. 107

5. Satsang or Socializing?

In the Sai Baba centers, it is important for us to understand the effects of our actions on others. There is an important difference between satsang and socializing. We have need for good company, but we must not allow our association to become mundane banter. Newcomers should be warmly welcomed, but members must avoid diluting the milk of satsang with the water of worldly affairs. We must maintain a spiritual focus in our discussion or we should be silent.

It is also important for us to know when we are providing good company for another, or the other is having a negative influence on us. Much introspection is required for us to be vigilant in the situation. We must know our own strengths and weaknesses very well. Even the highly evolved seeker is subject to the negative influence of bad company.

For the siddha (the accomplished seeker) too, one who has reached success, satsang is valuable, for it is like keeping a pot of water inside a tank of water: there will not be any loss by evaporation. If the yogi lives among worldly men, the chances of his yoga evaporating into bhoga (bad habits) are very great.

Sathya Sai Speaks 4, p. 226

Good company is important for the advanced aspirant, but it is even more important for the newcomer. When we are caught in the grips of worldly desire, we can only be reformed by good company. Without strong spiritual guidance and support we may not even realize our plight.

Join satsang, the company of the godly. Just as the tame elephants surround the wild tusker and rope him and bind him hand and foot and immobilize him before taming him, the spiritually minded will bring the doubter around.

Sathya Sai Speaks 2, p. 187

6. Resolve to Seek Only the Good

The choice is ours. We have clear decisions to make regarding our future: we can choose to do what is right or we can take the path of minimum effort. If we lose the opportunity to take the correct path now, can we be sure when the chance will come again?

Our heart is our best guide to correct action. It tells us if we are benefiting or losing from the company we keep. If we are inspired and uplifted, we feel the benefit. In good company all should profit from the shared spiritual energy and enthusiasm. The benefits of satsang can lead to liberation itself. Satsang enables us to see through the delusion of worldly desires. It can grant us a vision of our destination and a model for the journey.

Through satsang you develop freedom from delusion, through freedom from delusion you develop faith in truth, and through faith in truth you attain liberation itself.

Sathya Sai Speaks 10, p. 151

Questions for Study Circle

1. What is good company?

2. Why seek holy company?

3. Why does association have so much effect on people?

4. What is the difference between satsang and socializing?

5. How can we be a beneficial influence on others without their bad habits influencing us?

6. When is it better just to be alone?

7. Is it possible for us to remain unaffected by those around us?

8. Should we seek to change others?

9. Is satsang a spiritual discipline?

10. How do we practice the discipline of satsang in daily living?

References for Further Study

1. Gita Vahini, p. 224
2. Sathya Sai Speaks 6, p. 113 (The bear and the fly).
3. Sathya Sai Speaks 7, pp. 425-426.
4. Sathya Sai Speaks 8, pp. 210-213 (Friendship).
5. Sathya Sai Speaks 9, pp. 223-224.
6. Sathya Sai Speaks 10, p. 74, pp. 130-133.
7. Summer Showers 1973, pp. 47-56 (Who is a good man?).
8. Summer Showers 1973, p. 253.
9. Summer Showers 1977, pp. 246-247.
10. Summer Showers 1978, p. 89.
11. Summer Roses on the Blue Mountains, pp. 69-70.

Part Two: Deepening Understanding

CHAPTER TEN

Name: A Lantern in the Forest

1. The Power of Words

"In the beginning was the Word, and the Word was with God, and the Word was God." (Gospel of John, 1:1.)

In Christian, Hindu, and other religious traditions, the creation is described as originating from sound -- the Word of God. Sound is without form, taste, touch, or smell. It is the original manifestation of the creative process, having only the attributes of being enunciated and heard. Everything produces its own sound, for each being and object vibrates even to its own atomic level. The sound generated by an object tells us much about its nature and holds a key to its understanding. Religion has long recognized the importance of sound, particularly in the potency of the name of God.

The name of God holds great power, whether remembered silently or chanted aloud. Since the earliest days, remembrance and repetition of the name of God has been a potent spiritual discipline. Christians began to practice the repetition of the name of Jesus nineteen years after his crucifixion. [1] Meditative prayers centered on his name are widely practiced to this day in the Greek Orthodox and Russian Orthodox Churches and among Christians of other affiliations. In the time of the avatar Rama, divine words were said to have had the power to work miracles. Although people no longer rely on words for magical results, words are more important than ever. Today whole businesses and industries are devoted to processing and transmitting words. Clearly, words have great influence over all our lives.

---

1.   *Conversations, pg. 84*

Words have tremendous power. They can arouse emotions and they can calm them. They direct, they infuriate, they reveal, they confuse. They are potent forces that bring up great reserves of strength and wisdom. Therefore, have faith in the name and repeat it whenever you get the chance.
Sathya Sai Speaks 4, p. 184

2. Divine Names: Keys to Immortality

In this spiritual era, repetition of a divine name is a practice that is sufficient to endow us with spiritual liberation. Although the present age is characterized by spiritual decline, it is paradoxically the easiest time to gain release from the cycle of life and death. The Hindu scriptures speak of four great ages, or Yugas, each lasting many thousands of years. This age, the Kali Yuga, is marked by lack of virtue in social and individual life. However, because of the widespread wickedness among people, less is required of us to secure God's grace.

The present age is described in the sastras (sacred texts) as very conducive to liberation, for while in past ages rigorous penance was prescribed as the means, the Kali Age, in which you are, requires only namasmarana (remembrance of the name of the Lord) to win liberation!
Sathya Sai Speaks 4, p. 106

It is difficult to understand how such a simple practice can accomplish so much. A story is told that illustrates the point. A man stood beside a great forest at night and despaired. He had to cross through the forest in the darkness, but he held only a small lamp. He did not know how he would travel such a distance in the dark, because his lamp would light the path only a few feet ahead of him. While he despaired another traveler saw his plight. The second traveler explained that if he held the light before him it would show the path ahead as far as he needed to see.

Remembrance of the name is like that lamp. It guides our steps as far ahead as we need to see. Perhaps, like the traveler, we cannot see the solution because it is so simple.

Namasmarana is the best means. Only, you do not really believe that it can cure or save you: that is the tragedy. People believe in the efficacy of only costly, brightly packaged, widely published drugs; the simple, easily available remedy which is in everybody's backyard is ignored as useless.

Sathya Sai Speaks 2, pp. 164-165

3. Namasmarana, a Practice for All

From mountain solitudes and lonely jungles, the name of God has arisen from before recorded history. On shifting desert dunes and by timeless seas, his name has echoed into the vastness of creation. The practice of reciting the divine name can be taken up by anyone at any place in any time. There are no prerequisites for the discipline. It is the simplest and easiest path for our age.

For namasmarana, no expense is involved; no materials are needed; there is no special place or time to be provided. No qualification of scholarship or caste or sex has to be proved.

Sathya Sai Speaks 5, p. 80

Any name of God will shower grace, if repeated with sincerity and devotion. We need not renounce our own chosen form of God to engage in this practice. It is not restricted to one religion or to one name of God. We can choose any name that stirs love and joy within us. However, once a name is chosen, it should not be cast aside for a new name. If we decide to dig a well, we must continue to excavate in one spot. Many shallow holes will not yield the benefit of one deep hole.

The constant recital of the name of God -- any of the million names by which he is identified by human imagination or intelligence -- is the best means of correcting and cleansing the mind of man.

Sathya Sai Speaks 6, p. 133

4. Say the Name with Feeling

When a baby cries for its mother, she does not insist on correct pronunciation of her name; she immediately goes to the aid of her child. The child's longing and devotion to the mother draw her response. Thus, when we repeat the name of God we should say it with devotion and longing. The Lord sees the heart of the devotee and gauges the love and sincerity of the call. When we call on the Lord, we should visualize the form and picture the glory and sweetness of God.

> *The name of the Lord must be recited with awe and wonder, humility and reverence. The bow has to be drawn full before the arrow is released; then it will pierce the target. Feeling is the force that draws the string taut and makes the name reach the nami, the bearer of the name.*
>
> *Sathya Sai Speaks 4, p 165*

The divine name must be said with reverence. It must reflect our sincere yearning for unfoldment. Our actions must conform to our words. There is little use in reciting the name and expecting results if we are not living in accordance with high standards of conduct. Virtuous character and adherence to divine prescriptions for our behavior are essential ingredients.

> *The ajna or command of the guru or Lord is even more important than the name of the guru or the name of the Lord. Of what use is the repetition of the name without at the same time purifying the impulses by the observance of his commands?*
>
> *Sathya Sai Speaks 4, p. 47*

Very few spiritual teachers are capable of leading us to self-realization. Many teachers claim to know the path, but few demonstrate godly qualities. It is best to have faith in God and hold fast to him. God is our best guide for the current age. The most direct means to win his grace and guidance is through devotion and remembrance of his name. Only God can protect us in all circumstances and lead us to liberation.

The only hold that man has in this dreadful darkness is the name of God. That is the raft which will take him across this stormy sea darkened by hate and fear, churned by anxiety and terror.

Sathya Sai Speaks 6, p. 163

5. Have Faith in God's Wisdom and Mercy

When we climb aboard a train, we leave the task of reaching our destination to the engineer. He knows the method to direct the train through many junctions to its journey's end. We need only sit back and relax, enjoying the sights along the way. God will be the engineer of our lives if we have faith in him. He will himself direct our footsteps toward God-realization. The Lord knows our strengths and weaknesses. He can guide us along paths proper to our needs. We need only remember the Lord and have faith in his guidance.

The gardener alone knows how much earth to put under each plant and how the earth is to be so put. So, too, the order is "Do namasmarana!" Provided you continue that work, he himself will direct where and how the work is to be done.

Dhyana Vahini, p. 41

The Lord, in his infinite love and wisdom, determines what is required for our spiritual development. When we surrender to him, he guides and guards us. There is no need to worry or to resist his will.

Really, if you only have faith in the name, you need not struggle to secure the chance to detail to me your desires and wants. I will fulfill them, even without your telling me...Have the name bright and clear on your tongue, in your mind, and the Form symbolized by it before your eye and mental vision -- then nothing can harm you.

Sathya Sai Speaks 2, p. 165

6. Regular Practice Grants Success

If we wish to split a large rock, we may have to strike it with a hammer twenty-one times. The final blow that achieves success is dependent on the twenty unsuccessful attempts. Although no progress may be perceived until the final victory, all of our efforts to that point are essential.

Remembrance of God's name also may require repeated attempts, but no progress is lost. Whether seen or not, all efforts contribute to success. Complete surrender and faith in the Lord require constant effort. Results are not gained by superficial practice. The effort must be persistent and it must reflect our total devotion to achieving spiritual liberation.

> *The smarana (repetition of the name) has to be constant. If you rub a bit of iron on a hard surface, it develops heat. If you continue to rub it vigorously, it can be made red hot. If you do so between long intervals, the iron will become cold and all the effort up till then is a waste. The work has to be repeated over again.*
>
> *Sathya Sai Speaks 5, p. 275*

If developed fully, the practice of namasmarana enables us to win God's grace and reach the goal. Many people complain that they cannot find time for this exercise. However, they find time for activities of less importance. Time must also be found for this most worthwhile practice. However busy we are, we find time for the activities we consider to be essential.

> *You have no time for reciting the name of the Lord or meditating on his form, which is within you! Alas! You have time for the club, for a game of cards, for the film show, for wayside chats, for all kinds of trivialities, but no time for a little quiet, for a simple item like worship. It is a false excuse this, the want of time. No. Face the truth and proceed towards the truth.*
>
> *Sathya Sai Speaks 2, p. 168*

If we do not find time during our youth to remember the name, we may find it even more difficult to master the practice in old age. It is said that in our last moments, we should remember the name of the Lord. If we do so, we will gain liberation. However, to fix the mind on the Lord at the time of death requires great discipline and devotion throughout our lives. Those who do not take up the discipline in earnest now will be likely to fail when the moment arrives.

A story is told of a shopkeeper who named his seven sons each by a name of God. He knew that at the time of death he would call them; thus his last words would be the names of the Lord. When the shopkeeper's last moments arrived, he called all of his sons by their divine names as planned. However, when he realized that all of his sons were with him, he asked, "Who is minding the store?" and then he died. Thus he failed at the final moment, because his heart resided in his shop, not in God.[2]

7. The Name Is Enough

We may not command the spiritual power to rise in meditation to formless bliss. We may not possess the devotional heart that allows us to float in the warmth of the divine sea. We may be unable to perform the dedicated service that unfetters the chains of our actions. But if we hold fast to the name of God, we can still achieve fulfillment.

Constant remembrance of the name is a complete spiritual discipline. It fosters the virtues of devotion, patience, and faith. The practice grants us strength and confidence to travel the spiritual path to its conclusion. In time it can endow us with God-realization. Then we will know that the God we worship is within our own hearts, ever present and joyful.

The name is enough to give you all the results of every type of sadhana (spiritual discipline).

Sathya Sai Speaks 3, p. 15

Questions for Study Circle

1. Why does God's name hold such power?

2. Will any name of God do for recitation?

3. What is required to make the practice effective?

4. Does today's aspirant have enough time for remembrance of the name?

5. Is namasmarana too simple to be effective?

6. Is this a new spiritual discipline?

7. Is a special time or place necessary?

8. Can this practice by itself carry the seeker to spiritual realization?

9. Are words other than the Lord's name effective?

---

2. *Sathya Sai Speaks 1, pg. 7*

10. Do the words have to be said aloud?

11. How does a spiritual aspirant decide on a name?

References for Further Study

1. Conversations, pp. 84, 94-95, 119.

2. Dhyana Vahini, p. 36 (The name is better than the form).

3. Dhyana Vahini, pp. 37-39 (Benefits of namasmarana).

4. Dhyana Vahini, pp. 40-44.

5. Prema Vahini, p. 85 (Stay with one name).

6. Sanathana Sarathi, Aug. 1974, pp. 166-168.

7. Sandeha Nivarini, p. 5 (Keep one name).

8. Sathya Sai Speaks 1, pp. 35,85.

9. Sathya Sai Speaks 2, p. 7 (Remembrance at time of death).

10. Sathya Sai Speaks 3, pp. 14-18.

11. Sathya Sai Speaks 4, p. 216.

12. Sathya Sai Speaks 5, pp. 100-101.

13. Sathya Sai Speaks 6, pp. 200-201 (The name is like a precious gem).

14. Sathya Sai Speaks 6, pp. 280-281.

15. Sathya Sai Speaks 7, pp. 37-38 (How to use a japamala or rosary).

16. Sathya Sai Speaks 7, pp. 123-124 (Why divine names have two syllables).

17. Sathya Sai Speaks 10, pp. 70-71 (The officer and the teacher).

CHAPTER ELEVEN

Prayer: Let's Talk

1. Does Prayer Really Work?

Yes, prayer works- but not always in the manner we intend. We may not receive a particular benefit that we seek, but prayer still draws us closer to God. It establishes a line of communication with the Lord and builds his presence in our minds. And yes, many times our specific prayers are granted--although not always as we expect.

Prayer is a key which opens many doors. Whether we are giving thanks or seeking help for ourselves or others, we are working to understand our relationship with the Lord. Some prayers are praises to God, some are affirmations of his glory, some are petitions for help, and some are prayers of thanksgiving, but in all prayers we seek to draw closer to God. Prayer is one of the most basic and most ancient elements of every religion -- a model of positive thinking.

> *Prayer is the very breath of religion, for it brings man and God together and with every sigh, nearer and nearer.*
> *Sathya Sai Speaks 7, p. 291*

2. How Do We Start?

When we begin our new spiritual life, our desires are like a runaway train. It is impossible to stop them immediately. We can only redirect them along channels which reduce the risk to ourselves and others. If we switch the train to an uphill track, it will gradually lose its momentum and we can regain control. Prayer is the uphill track for our runaway desires. Until we direct our aspirations along proper lines, it is best to steer them to God. The Lord knows what is best for us; he will help us to direct our efforts along the right lines.

From the very outset it is necessary for us to practice the habit of regular prayer. A regular time and place for prayer help us to quickly concentrate and reach a state of calm. Regular prayer makes us aware of God's omnipresence and attracts his grace, for God is as close to us as we are to him.

At the beginning, one might need some special set of circumstances for clearing the mind for concentration on God. But after a while, if one finds that God is omnipresent and becomes aware of him and one's thoughts are centered on God, then no matter where one is, it is the same. Prayers may be addressed to God and the prayers will reach him.

Conversations, p. 43

God knows what we seek, but it is up to us to ask. In asking we make a conscious choice of what path we wish to follow. We ask for specific results and thereby accept the consequences of those results.

It is your duty to ask God. Words must be said, and the words must correspond to the thought. The thought must be put into a true word. It is true enough that the divinity knows all, but he requires that the true word be said. The mother may know that to maintain life the child requires food, but milk is given when the child asks for it.

Conversations, p. 42

We must ask for what we want, but our actions should not contradict our words. If we pray for greater love, we cannot continue to harbor hate. If we long for humility, we cannot continue to strut about in pride. When we pray, we must also do our part to fulfill the request. We cannot receive grace before we have made our own best effort to secure our objective. Our thoughts, words, and deeds must all support our prayer.

Prayer must be united with practice. You should not pray for one thing and practice another. Such prayer is only a means of deception. The words you utter, the deeds you do, the prayers you make must all be directed along the same path.

Prasanthi Vahini, p. 34

No one can instruct another when or how that person should pray. All of us have different needs and attitudes. What is appropriate at one time may not be at another time. The values and languages of different cultures also vary. It is not possible for us to evaluate the worth of another person's prayer, for all speak to God in their own ways. It is not the words we use or the form of God we address that gives prayer its power: it is the devotion in our hearts.

The stamp of bhakti (devotion) is what makes the prayer reach the destination, God; not the festoons, the fanfare, the heap of flowers, or the festive nature of the feast-offerings. The simple, sincere heart is the stamp that makes the prayer travel fast.

Sathya Sai Speaks 7, p. 259

Prayers are not always answered immediately. Many of us wish for one thing today and for another thing tomorrow. We must show that our prayer is a heartfelt need. It must be sincere and pure to reach the Lord.

Prayers for worldly ends do not reach God. They will reach only those deities who deal with such restricted spheres. But all prayers arising from pure love, unselfish eagerness to render service, and from hearts that are all-inclusive will reach God.

Sathya Sai Speaks 11, p. 68

3. What Should We Pray for?

In prayer we need not request anything at all. Prayer may be best used simply to draw us closer to God -- to bring God into our lives and attract his grace. Prayer can then enable us to experience the joy and bliss which God confers.

Our devotion and prayer to God should not be for the sole purpose of obtaining something or fulfilling some desire of ours. This should be for the sake of atma (the inner divinity) and for the sake of becoming one with the Lord and for the sake of getting the bliss that one can get by being close to the Lord.

Summer Showers 1974, p. 176

It is best to pray for results which reduce desires and promote peace, love, and understanding. These are the proper objects of prayer; they are the special gifts of God which are not available in any shop. Perhaps the wisest object of prayer is for the removal of the obstacles which block our spiritual progress. Persistence may be required for us to obtain our goal, but tenacious effort builds spiritual strength. The difficulty of our journey sometimes grants us added fortitude, as the strongest steel is forged in fire. If we listen to our loving hearts, not to the rationalizations of our minds, we will concentrate on proper goals. The heart is a wiser guide and is the source of true prayer and communion with God.

Prayers must emanate from the heart, where God resides,
and not from the head, where doctrines and doubts clash.
                                    Sathya Sai Speaks 7, p. 83

It is important to pray for benefits which further spiritual progress. When we experience difficulty in fulfilling our wishes, it may be that we need to examine and possibly change our attitude rather than present circumstances. Many times the things for which we pray are obstacles to our spiritual progress. In fact, it may be best for us that most of our prayers are not granted. It is not always possible for us to determine the consequences of our desires. The following story illustrates this point.

A young man once had a simple wish: he prayed for a job so that he could leave his parents' home. Next, he prayed for a wife to cook for him and provide a home for him. With the wife came children, so he prayed for a big house to put them in and a car to carry his family around town. Then he needed a better job to support all of his obligations. Finally the poor fellow was so burdened by his many responsibilities that he only wished to retire into the forest alone to meditate. Unfortunately his spiritual prayer could not be granted, because all of his previous prayers for material benefits had been granted.

God gives you whatever you pray for, so take care. Ask for
the right things.
                                    Sathya Sai Speaks 3, p. 230

It is best to let the Lord decide what we should receive. He sees the past, the present, and the future of us all. The material objects that we pray for often increase our desires and make our lives more difficult. However, some material wishes may be granted so that we will appreciate God's benevolence. Swami says: "I give you what you want, so that you will learn to want what I have to give." Still, the wise course is to trust in the Lord to provide what is necessary for us.

Not knowing what we should ask, we are asking him for
something when really we want something else. In this
process, we are getting ourselves into difficulties. God is
always ready to give you all that you want, but you do not
seem to know what is good for you and what you really want.
Since you do not know what you should want and under
what circumstances, it is better and easier to surrender
yourself completely to God and simply ask for his grace.
                                    Summer Showers 1973, p. 134

4. The Answer Will Come When the Time Is Right

It is beyond us to know how or why prayers are granted. So many factors are involved that we cannot hope to understand the process. Timing, karma, grace, the degree of personal effort -- all have a bearing on the situation.

There may be other reasons why our prayers are not answered. We may have karma to work out or lessons to learn. When we pray for a miraculous cure, we may not see the factors which caused the illness. Some people receive cures, while others do not. If the lessons of that illness have not been learned, it would be cruel to relieve the illness, for it would only have to be repeated. But if the lessons have been learned and the debt paid, then a cure could endow the aspirant with new faith and determination.

It is always wisest for us to put our trust in the Lord. He takes care of our needs without being asked when we try to live a good life and dedicate our actions to him. God is our eternal parent; he cares for his children and tries to direct them in beneficial directions.

> *If a bhakta (devotee) has dedicated his all -- body, mind, and existence -- to the Lord, the Lord will himself look after everything, for he will always be with the bhakta. Under such conditions, there is no need for prayer. But have you so dedicated yourself and surrendered everything to the Lord?*
> *Prasanthi Vahini, p. 14*

It is easier for us to learn how to live in the world than to change it to meet our expectations. We cannot expect immediate fulfillment of our many desires. Through prayer we learn to accept that which we cannot change and to change what we can. However, some prayers do not even require an answer, while others may take a lifetime to realize.

Questions for Study Circle

1. What is the function of prayer?
2. How many kinds of prayer are there?
3. Why are some prayers answered and others are not?
4. Should we pray for results or leave events up to God?
5. What makes prayer effective?

6. Is a regular time and place for prayer necessary?

7. What obstacles may keep prayers from being answered?

8. Does God hear all prayers?

9. What are worthy objects of prayer?

10. How long should we wait for an answer?

11. Are traditional prayers more effective than spontaneous prayers?

References for Further Study

1. Sanathana Sarathi, Sept. 1979, pp. 193-194 (All prayers do not go directly to God).

2. Conversations, p. 42.

3. Eastern View of Jesus, p. 26-27.

4. Summer Showers 1979, p. 8 (Some prayers are handled by God's "ministers").

5. We Devotees, p. 162.

CHAPTER TWELVE

Meditation: Search for the Divinity Within

1. What Is Meditation?

Meditation is a word with many meanings. To some, meditation is a science of the mind. To others, it is an art, indefinable and mystical. For almost all, it is difficult to understand. Meditation denotes quiet introspection or absorption in the divine. It means exploring and expanding consciousness. Meditation can be the awakening of inner energies or the discovery of self-understanding. It may be repeating the name of the Lord with love, or simply collecting oneself for the day ahead. To all, meditation is a means to concentrate within, to discover the inner wellsprings of love and wisdom, of joy and peace.

Meditation for spiritual aspirants is a practice of inner contemplation. Its goal is the realization of Oneness in the world and in ourselves. The practice transforms us and our perspective of the world. With time, meditation may grant us ultimate self-understanding. We come to see ourselves and the creation as manifestations of God's will. The illusion of separateness disappears when all is experienced as One.

> *Real meditation is getting absorbed in God as the only thought, the only goal. God only, only God. Think God, breathe God, love God, live God.*
>
> *Conversations, p. 133*

The basic method of meditation is to rise above thought to the source of thought. The destination is a state of being beyond the mental process. God cannot be understood by means of rational explanation or argument, but by experiential knowledge alone.

> *As long as one knows he is meditating, one is not meditating. In that absorption in God, one puts aside every form and merges in God. In that process the mind naturally stops.*
>
> *Conversations, p. 133*

Meditation enables us to transcend the intellect. There is nothing for us to "know" in a rational sense. Actually, what is accomplished is a state of equanimity in which our divine nature has an opportunity to manifest itself. For we already possess divinity within; we need only to become aware of it and to allow it to emerge and express itself. When that happens, an inner transformation is achieved. That transformation results in joy and peace beyond description.

> *Dhyana (meditation) is synonymous with the unitive knowlege of the Godhead. It is...a vision of and path to the divine. It leads to...the integral reality of existence-consciousness-bliss (sat-chit-ananda).*
>
> *Summer Showers 1979, p. 101*

Meditation methods, techniques, and goals vary widely among aspirants and disciples. Some aspirants prefer an intense regimen; others enjoy a more leisurely practice. Some aspirants welcome a fixed time and place for meditation; for others, an unexpected lull in the day may be more beneficial, even in a crowded or noisy place. There is no one way to meditate that precludes all others. Each person must find their own method.

> *Can anyone train another in meditation? Or claim to train? It may be possible to teach a person the posture, the pose, the position of the legs, feet, or hands, neck, head or back, the style of breathing or its speed. But meditation is a function of the inner man; it involves deep subjective quiet, the emptying of the mind and filling oneself with the light that emerges from the divine spark within. This is a discipline that no textbook can teach and no class can communicate.*
>
> *Sathya Sai Speaks 7, p. 356*

2. How Do We Start?

If you have ever gazed with wonder at a star-filled night or marveled at the miracle of a wildflower, you have already begun. Everyone is traveling the path to God, but some are more aware of the journey than others. Some of us drift on a lazy tide, while others rocket toward the destination as if guided by a compass.

Direction is an essential element. We must be guided by one who already knows the way. If we strike out on our own, we may also reach the goal, but the journey will be more difficult. Many aspirants have tested the directions of Sathya Sai Baba and have recognized the guideposts of joy and love along the way. By carefully listening to the instructions of Sai Baba and the indications of our heart, we can discern the proper path for ourselves. The instruction is genuine, but we must reflect within to understand how we can practice the principles in our own lives. Beginning meditation serves this purpose -- to help us understand and practice holy teachings.

One method, which Sathya Sai Baba describes as the most universal and effective, is the light meditation. [1] To practice this meditation, Swami recommends that the aspirant set aside a few minutes every day, preferably in the morning before the events of the day distract the mind. A small lamp or candle can be used to help the meditator visualize the light of love and truth. This flame is pictured between the eyebrows as the light of wisdom; from there it is brought down to the heart and visualized as a lotus of love blooming petal by petal. As the light grows, it purifies all the senses and impulses, taking all into the light of divine love. Over time, this meditation purifies the individual's thoughts and actions, making him or her fit for realization of divinity.

Meditation is naturally difficult at first. Most people cater to the needs of the body first and neglect the spirit. The process must be reversed so that the body serves the indweller. The mind must become master of the senses. When the mind asserts control over the senses, the process of self-mastery begins.

> *There are some who while meditating strike at the mosquitos that pester them! No, immerse yourselves in dhyanam (meditation) until you transcend all physical and mental urges and impulses.*
>
> *Sathya Sai Speaks 4, p. 236*

Meditation requires us to explore within, a place not too many are familiar with. Particularly in the West, we are accustomed to seeking satisfaction outside of ourselves. It is not so common for us to look

---

1.   *Sathya Sai Speaks 6, pp.239-240*

within for peace and happiness. However, with regular practice, meditation becomes a joyful, even indispensable part of each day. In the beginning, it is important for us to create a regular habit of meditation. A fixed time and place help us to dive within more quickly. Patience and tenacity are required to establish the habit.

> *For meditation to be effective, there must be steady practice with no hurry or worry. With steady practice, the person will become quiet and the state of meditation will naturally come about.*
>
> *Conversations, p. 139*

Real meditation promotes the constant awareness that all activity carries us closer to God. It is useless for us to elevate our thoughts in meditation if in the next moment we give way to pride or criticism. We must maintain one-pointed awareness and commitment to our liberation. All of our activities should reflect our appreciation of the omnipresent divinity.

> *In real dhyana, you soon get over the consciousness that you are doing dhyana. In fact, every moment in life must be utilized for dhyana. That is the best way to live. When you sweep your rooms clean, tell yourselves that your hearts too have to be swept likewise. When you cut vegetables, feel that lust and greed too have to be cut into pieces. When you press chapathis (flat Indian bread) wider and wider, desire in addition that your love may take in wider and wider circles and expand even into the regions of strangers and foes.*
>
> *Sathya Sai Speaks 6, p. 298*

When constant meditation is practiced, there cannot be only one posture or one prescribed method of concentration. We can meditate while we walk, while we drive, or during our other quiet times. The inner subjective state is important, not the outer circumstances. Our inner needs dictate the pace and manner of practice.

> *Sitting in meditation, the question often comes up, "How long should we sit?" There is no answer. There is no particular time. Meditation is really an all-day-long process.*
>
> *Conversations, p. 57*

3. How Can We Recognize Progress?

A miner knows success when he strikes gold. A racer knows success when he crosses the finish line. A meditator knows success when he transforms his character. Meditation must enable us to practice truthfulness, love, inner peace, and care for all beings. If meditation cannot change our lives, it is a hollow practice. If we do not have the conviction to act on our inner direction, we waste our time in listening for the voice. If we do not practice our duty, we are only putting on a show for ourselves or others. What is the use of sitting in meditation if no result is achieved?

> *Do you love more, do you talk less, do you serve others more earnestly? These are the signs of success in dhyana. Your progress must be authenticated by your character and behavior.*
>
> *Sathya Sai Speaks 7, p. 30*

True meditation helps us discover our inner identity. It enables us to hear the divine voice in our heart, which illumines the path ahead. It allows us to perceive and develop divine qualities.

> *Man is divine. He can purify himself into perfect divinity by the process of dhyana, taken up with eagerness and followed with faith by virtuous individuals.*
>
> *Sathya Sai Speaks 6, p. 239*

Progress in meditation results in the elimination of desire. Desire gives us no peace; instead, it hides the divine light in our hearts. When the mind is controlled and examined, it is seen to have no form of its own. Like a shining mirror, it only assumes the image of that which is reflected in it. Our object must be to see directly the light of the atma, the inner divinity, without the aid of this mirror. To do this, we must remove desire.

> *The mind has no independent identity of its own; it is a conglomeration of the desires that sprout from the impulses. A cloth is essentially a bundle of threads. Threads, in their truth, are basically cotton. Similarly, desires arise from basic impulses, and the mind is constituted of these desires. Just as a piece of cloth disintegrates if threads in it are pulled apart, the mind too can be destroyed by the eradication of desires.*
>
> *Summer Showers 1979, p. 116*

4. Make Joy Your Priceless Possession

Would a miner leave a rich vein of gold in the ground? Would a thief leave behind riches and take only trash? Would a diver drop a pearl and take only sand? Then why do we settle for the tinsel of the world while the greatest treasure lies untapped within us?

The personality and body, which we take to be ourselves, is only a passing phenomenon. Through meditation, we must discern the real from the unreal, the passing from the permanent, the valuable from the worthless. The reality is God within each person. He is omnipresent, manifesting himself as love and joy beyond understanding. The goal of meditation must be to realize that joyful vision. Repetition of the name is one of its most effective techniques.

By means of dhyana, you can realize that I am the resident in all hearts, the urge, the motive, the guide, the goal. Yearn for that vision, that awareness, and make it your priceless possession.

Sathya Sai Speaks 7, pp. 473-474

Questions for Study Circle

1. What is the purpose of meditation?

2. What are the benefits of meditation?

3. Is meditation essential for spiritual progress?

4. Is one type of meditation best?

5. Can meditation be taught?

6. How do we learn to meditate?

7. Is meditation a mental process?

8. How can progress in meditation be evaluated?

9. Can we progress spiritually through meditation alone?

References for Further Study

1. Bhagavad Gita, Chapter 6.

2. Conversations, p. 72 (Visions of Swami in meditation are real).

3. Conversations, pp. 132-145.

4. Dhyana Vahini, p. 7 (Method).

5. Dhyana Vahini, p. 14 (Success in meditation is proportionate to right conduct).

6. Dhyana Vahini, p. 18 (Equal-mindedness).

7. Sathya Sai Speaks 1, pp. 34-36.

8. Sathya Sai Speaks 5, p. 30 (Dreams of Swami are real).

9. Sathya Sai Speaks 6, pp. 239-241 (Light meditation).

10. Sathya Sai Speaks 7, p. 120 (Seven states of meditation).

11. Sathya Sai Speaks 9, p. 33 (Kundalini yoga).

12. Sathya Sai Speaks 9, pp. 185-186 (Concentration, contemplation, and meditation).

13. Sathya Sai Speaks 10, pp. 117-119 (Chakras).

14. Sathya Sai Speaks 10, p. 152 (Evidence of progress in meditation).

15. Sathya Sai Speaks 10, p. 248 (Merging of thoughts in God).

16. Sathya Sai Speaks 10, p. 273 (Types of meditation).

17. Summer Showers 1979, pp. 80-84.

18. Summer Showers 1979, pp. 99-103 (States of consciousness).

19. Summer Showers 1979, p. 103 (Supernormal experiences).

20. Summer Showers 1979, pp. 111-112, 115.

CHAPTER THIRTEEN

Grace: How Sweet It Is

1. What Is Grace?

Spiritual grace is a benefit bestowed by God. It is a transformation of attitude or events that helps us to draw closer to realizing our divine nature. Grace grants us opportunities to avoid wasted time and trouble while on the spiritual path. It may manifest as wisdom or inspiration or material aid. The result can appear in any form.

> *Grace will set everything right. Its main consequence is "self-realization," but there are other incidental benefits, too, like a happy, contented life here below and a cool, courageous temper, established in unruffled equanimity...This is the nature of grace. It fulfills a variety of wants.*
>
> *Sathya Sai Speaks 6, p. 184*

2. How Do We Get Grace?

In remote areas of New England, travelers to rustic lanes are sometimes bewildered by local attitudes. On asking directions to their destination, they have sometimes received the reply, "You can't get there from here." Fortunately, there is always a way when we search in the correct direction. The journey to spiritual grace is also possible if we ask the right questions and enlist the right guide.

Some divine benefits are available to all who are receptive. It is our birthright to receive God's love and aid. When we walk the razor's edge, we become particularly aware of the light and love which protect us.

> *God's grace is as the shower of rain, as the sunlight. You have to do some sadhana (spiritual practice) to acquire it: the sadhana of keeping a pot upright to receive the rain, the sadhana of opening the door of your heart so that the sun may illumine it.*
>
> *Sathya Sai Speaks 6, p. 184*

The use we make of our gifts determines the benefit we receive. We are free to act according to our own will. We can use our gifts for the benefit of others or toward their downfall. The quality of our motivation colors the results we achieve.

> *Water in lakes, pits, wells, and rivers is rain water, though the taste, color, name, and form are different, based on where the rain has fallen and how pure the container is. Divine grace is like rain, pure, pellucid, falling on all. How it is received and used depends on the heart of man.*
>
> *Sathya Sai Speaks 4, p. 18*

When we live a good life, grace follows us automatically. No special request is required. The divine energy flows naturally to those who love and serve others. As water naturally fills lakes and streams, grace flows spontaneously to one living in accordance with spiritual principles.

> *If a person has a pure heart and is living Swami's teachings, Swami's grace is automatic. No karma can prevent that.*
>
> *Conversations, p. 109*

There are two types of grace: that which is earned and that which is unearned. Grace from God may be bestowed at a particular time in our lives as a result of past meritorious actions. Or it may be an unearned gift from the Lord based on our spiritual progress and devotion. Of course, we do not know which type of grace we have received, if we realize we have received grace at all.

> *You can draw checks on a bank only when you have deposited therein, or you can mortgage your property and take a loan, or the bank may grant you an overdraft. The property on which you can take a loan is the "accumulated merit consequent on the good deeds of previous lives." The overdraft on which you can draw in times of emergency is grace, which God showers when you are sincere and steady enough to deserve it. You must give some surety or someone as security to get a loan: the surety is divine grace; the security is the fixity of your faith, the solidarity of your surrender.*
>
> *Sathya Sai Speaks 7, p. 175*

The principal means to earn grace is by dedicated and unruffled spiritual practice. Dedicated practice is achieved by reforming our character along the lines of right conduct and developing love for all.

When we purify our character, we become increasingly fit to receive grace.

> *Above all, try to win grace by reforming your habits, reducing your desires, and refining your higher nature. One step makes the next one easier; that is the excellence of the spiritual journey. At each step, your strength and confidence increase and you get bigger and bigger installments of grace.*
>
> *Sathya Sai Speaks 5, p. 30*

To master the art of self-transformation, we must start early. The journey is easier and more enjoyable when we plan sufficient time for the road. To win grace, we should begin, if possible, while still young. If we waste youth in pursuit of sensuous desires, who will listen to our cries when we reach old age? The fear of death and sickness causes many to think of God, but who thinks of God when life is pleasant and new? The difficulty of the path makes an early start highly desirable.

> *If at an advanced age you try to control your desires and senses, you may or may not win the Lord's grace. On the other hand, if at this young age you control your sense organs, there is no doubt whatsoever that you will gain God's grace.*
>
> *Summer Showers 1973, p. 138*

But before we call for the grace of the Lord, we must first use all of our own abilities to help ourselves. If we call on the Lord before we have used the means already at our disposal, we are being lazy. We must first make our best effort to solve our own problems.

> *When you have done your best and that is found not enough, then call on me. I am ever ready to reinforce your exertions with my grace.*
>
> *Sathya Sai Speaks 2, p. 123*

When we act in accordance with the call of the divine inner voice, the journey becomes easier. Spiritual development makes each step more certain and the goal appears closer. Less effort is required as beneficial habits are reinforced. As we taste the sweetness of the tonic, our practice of discipline becomes more pleasurable. We become confident of our own abilities and grace flows to us automatically.

Individual effort and divine grace are both interdependent. Without effort, there will be no conferment of grace. Without grace, there can be no gain from the effort. To win that grace, you need have only faith and virtue.

Sathya Sai Speaks 5, p. 188

By practicing selfless love, we identify directly with God. Practicing love for man and God is the most potent means to earn grace. God is love and is drawn by love. Love purifies us so that we may recognize and receive grace.

The grace of God cannot be won through the gymnastics of reason, the contortions of yoga, or the denials of asceticism. Love alone can win it, love that needs no requital, love that knows no bargaining, love that is paid gladly as tribute to the All-Loving, love that is unwavering. Love alone can overcome obstacles, however many and mighty.

Sathya Sai Speaks 7, p. 459

3. How Does Grace Appear?

Sometimes grace does not appear in a form that we may recognize. It may arrive unseen, like the sweet dew at dawn. Grace may burst upon us like waves in a torrent of joy, or it may knock at our door wearing a disguise -- a blessing hidden in the clothes of misfortune.

Grace manifests in many ways. Protection from accidents or disasters is one of the most startling ways in which it might appear. But we may not always be aware when we have been saved from calamity. We do not know what losses or injuries we might have suffered but for divine intervention.

Through steady spiritual practice we may have earned unknown respite from at least some of the results of our past actions. Many instances are recorded of devotees who have been saved from obvious and imminent disaster by Sathya Sai Baba. Such is the power of the Lord's grace and the importance of following his precepts. Baba protects and guides his devotees safely along the surest path.

The most desirable form of wealth is the grace of God. He will guard you, even as the lids guard the eye. Do not doubt this.

Sathya Sai Speaks 4, p. 190

Many obstacles to our spiritual progress are better overcome than avoided. Only when an obstacle is surmounted may we pass to the next test. The course of events is best left to the Lord. He knows the safest course for each aspirant. If we rely on the Lord, we will come to no harm.

Rely on the grace of God; earn it and keep it. Then whatever the strength of the storm, you can survive it without harm.
Sathya Sai Speaks 4, p. 364

Divine grace does not always appear when or as we might wish. When we strive to advance spiritually, we must confront the obstacles which block our way. The best course may be to experience the pain or suffering, which cleanses us. The process may be painful, but sometimes pain benefits us the most.

It is grace. Those who suffer have my grace. Only through suffering will they be persuaded to turn inward and make the inquiry. And without turning inward and making inquiry, they can never escape misery.
Conversations, p. 110

When grace affords us an opportunity to atone for past actions, we may experience pain and loss. However, the grace of God lessens the pain and reduces the loss. The suffering may be essential for our growth and so we must experience it. The Lord's grace reduces our burden.

When a severe pain torments you, the doctor gives you a morphine injection and you do not feel the pain, though it is there in the body. Grace is like the morphine: the pain is not felt, though you go through it! Grace takes away the malignity of the karma which you have to undergo...
Sathya Sai Speaks 4, p. 154

Although the burden of past actions may have to be endured, the grace of God minimizes the pain, or may even eliminate it. Karma is not an insurmountable obstacle. When we exert our best efforts, the Lord reduces the obstacle to a size that we can bear.

You may say that the burden of past acts and their inevitable consequences have to be borne, but the grace of the Lord can burn that burden in a flash...
Sathya Sai Speaks 4, p. 356

Grace may manifest in the devotee as noble or virtuous character. Such character is the most important grace to obtain. Without it all good fortune would yield little benefit. The greatest grace is that which makes us virtuous -- and selflessly loving.

> *No more can any faculty of yours hinder your progress. He will orient all of your faculties towards the highest goal: the senses, the mind, the subconscious, the unconscious, the intelligence -- all. Grace will confer all you need.*
>
> *Sathya Sai Speaks 6, p. 76*

4. Grace: Without It There Is Neither Start Nor Finish

Most people are lost in a waking dream. They wander about believing the real to be false and the false to be real. Like absent-minded actors in a play, they have forgotten their lines and they take their haphazardly improvised role to be reality. Without grace, one cannot even start the Lord's play, much less bow at the finale.

The grace of God is essential for "salvation." It helps us to grow in many ways, granting more than we could ask for. Not even the urge to realize divinity can be obtained without God's grace. The means, the ability, and our achievement of the goal are all dependent upon grace.

> *Through the grace of the Lord alone can man develop a desire for advaita, or nonduality of the universe, one without second.*
>
> *Sathya Sai Speaks 6, p. 170*

All our efforts should be directed toward winning God's grace. His grace is our only true wealth. It is our greatest possession in this life and the next. Without that grace, there can be little sweetness in our lives.

> *God's grace is the greatest wealth. To consider the amassing of money, gold, or other material objects as symbols of wealth and social prestige is incorrect. The goal of life, instead, should be the acquisition of the divine wealth of God's grace.*
>
> *Summer Showers 1979, p. 152*

Questions for Study Circle

1. What is grace?
2. Does grace always make life easier?
3. Can grace overcome any obstacle?
4. How is grace earned?
5. Can grace be an unearned gift?
6. How do we know if we have received grace?
7. In what form may grace arrive?
8. Why does God grant grace?
9. How does God decide who should receive grace?
10. If you could, what grace would you grant yourself?

References for Further Study

1. An Eastern View of Jesus, pp. 18-19.
2. Conversations, pp. 111-112.
3. Jnana Vahini, p. 67 (With grace, one can have a vision of the atma, however deficient one is in other areas).
4. Sanathana Sarathi, Jan. 1985, p. 12.
5. Sathya Sai Speaks 4, p. 128 (The man who called for the Lord's help, but did not make his own effort).
6. Sathya Sai Speaks 6, p. 184.
7. Sathya Sai Speaks 7, p. 26 (Grace is won by effort).
8. Sathya Sai Speaks 7, p. 162-163 (Good deeds may be drawn on like bank credit).
9. Sathya Sai Speaks 7, pp. 196 (Earn grace by doing the Lord's will).
10. Sathya Sai Speaks 7, pp. 470-471.
11. Sathya Sai Speaks 9, p. 226 (Four stages of acquiring grace).
12. Sathya Sai Speaks 10, p. 228 (Win grace by purity of heart and mastery of senses).

13. Summer Showers 1974, p. 183 (Grace depends on nearness to God).

14. Summer Showers 1974, p. 255 (Without love, God's grace cannot flow).

15. We Devotees, p. 54.

CHAPTER FOURTEEN

Truth: More Fundamental than the Atom

1. The Unchanging Absolute

Ultimate truth is unchanging, pure, and eternal. It is the anchor that saves the ship tossed by high seas. It is the pole star that guides our journey in darkest night. Always faithful, truth sustains and guides us at all times.

Truth is never far, for it is the nature of the atma. It resides within, awaiting our call. When we recognize our divine truth, the atma, the unity and grandeur of life begin to flower before our eyes. Truth manifests in action as dharma, spiritual obligation. It expresses itself in being as love and purity of heart. Eternal truth knows no distinctions of culture or time. It is ever-unchanging, unmoved, unaffected.

> *Truth is something that is not modified by time or space or guna (attribute). It must be the same forever, unaffected and unchanged; then alone is it truth. It should not be proved false by some subsequent event or knowledge.*
>
> *Sathya Sai Speaks 3, p. 116*

The material world is ever-changing. The phenomenal plane is characterized by maya, illusion. Illusion causes the unity of God to appear diverse and mutable. It causes Oneness to appear as many. Unchanging truth is experienced only in the purified consciousness. It is not characteristic of appearance in this world.

> *Nothing is absolutely true, really real. The waking experience is as unreal as the dream experience. When you are in deep sleep, there is no world at all. When you attain the superconscious fourth stage, the "I" alone remains, the universal "I" which was mistaken even in the sleeping stage as limited and particular.*
>
> *Sathya Sai Speaks 4, p. 97*

2. Can We Know Truth?

We believe we can know truth because the saints and sages have experienced and described it. We search for it with the spotlight of faith. Sathya Sai Baba tells us that the search for truth is the purpose of human life. With the tools of dedication, devotion, and love, we follow its footprints left in the soft earth of our experience.

Yes, truth can be found. Its signs are everywhere: in our eyes, in our ears, in our hearts. When we drink from the wellspring of the heart, we taste its nectar straight from the source. Through spiritual search, God's grace is procured and the goal achieved.

> *The chief duty of man is investigation into truth. Truth can be won only through dedication and devotion, and they are dependent on the grace of God, which is showered on hearts saturated with love.*
>
> *Sathya Sai Speaks 6, p. 1*

Spiritual truth is the bedrock on which life's foundation rests. Our capacity to experience and practice some effective degree of truth provides us with our best guide through life. We alone among all God's creatures can discern our truth and the truth of creation.

> *Truth is more fundamental than the atom. Every atom and every star manifests the truth to those who have the eye of wisdom...What is the special feature of man? If he too lives and dies as any animal, how can his supremacy be justified? His supremacy lies in his capacity to become aware of his truth.*
>
> *Sathya Sai Speaks 10, pp. 126-127*

3. How Do We Practice Truth?

Divine truth is like a flame. When it contacts the dry tinder of a person's life, it spreads and grows strong. When it touches the green wood of doubt and desire, it only hisses and smokes. To experience universal truth, we must start by lighting the small flame of relative truth. If we begin by practicing truthfulness of speech, we initiate the transformation. A story illustrates the transforming power of truthfulness.

A thief was convinced by a holy man to adhere to truth. A short time later, during a burglary of the king's palace, the thief was confronted by another man. He invited his new companion to share in the spoils of the royal treasury. After emptying the vaults, they parted company, leaving behind a sole diamond for the bereaved king. The thief's companion asked him where he lived, to which the thief had to reply truthfully.

The following day, the break-in was discovered by the royal minister, and the king convened an inquiry. The king accused the royal minister of the theft of the single diamond -- for the king had been the companion of the truthful thief. The thief was appointed as the new minister and his adherence to truth and justice became noted in the land.

If we adhere to truth, we will be saved. Truth protects and promotes the welfare of its adherents. If we hold fast to truth we serve our own best interests.

> *Have faith that truth will save you in the long run. Stick to it regardless of what might befall.*
>
> *Sathya Sai Speaks 1, p. 48*

If we remain open to truth, our success is assured. The difficulty of the journey for us is to constantly seek a higher truth, not being satisfied until reality is perceived. As we climb the mountain of truth, we must continue to look for the higher summits of the range. Our natural tendency is to be satisfied with the limited truth we have found, so that we can relax our inquiry. However, we must be willing to continue our search until realization is attained. When self-understanding is gained, there is no more doubt.

> *Man has doubt only when he does not know the truth. Once you experience the truth, doubt will vanish. Truth is One, and for all time truth is truth. Whatever changes, know that as untruth.*
>
> *Conversations, p. 2*

Truth in our lives must be a twofold path: it must be sought within and also experienced through selfless practice in the world. Truth should be the constant motivator of our actions. Through correct action, we remove karmic obstacles and gain the Lord's grace. We must also pursue inner truth in meditation. A broad and unfettered mind is required for self-realization. The mind must be open and without preconceptions; then alone will it be fit for realization.

To discover this truth, the classic texts have laid down two codes of discipline, one external and the other internal -- the outer and the inner. The outer is nishkama-karma (activity that is engaged in as dedication and worship; activity that is gladly carried out from a sense of duty regardless of the benefit that may accrue, with no attachment to the fruits thereof). The inner is dhyana (meditation on the splendor of which one is but a spark). Karma or activity has to be regulated by dharma (righteousness), then it will lead one to Brahman (the basic truth of the universe, including Oneself).

Sathya Sai Speaks 6, p. 189

We must adhere to truth, but we must be careful how we express it. We should not intentionally hurt another person. A truth spoken at the wrong time and place may do as much damage as an untruth. We must remember that God dwells in all people and that loving understanding is an essential part of truth.

Speak the truth, but speak pleasantly. Simply because a statement will be welcome to the hearer, don't speak it out to win his approval; if speaking truth will cause grief or pain, keep silent. That is the vow of truth in ordinary daily life. Don't have hypocrisy or crookedness in your speech. Both unpleasant truth and pleasant untruth have to be avoided.

Sathya Sai Speaks 6, p. 128

4. Love, the Highest Truth

The wave cannot be separated from the ocean. The sun cannot be removed from its heat and light. Neither can love be separated from truth. They are eternal companions. They do not travel without each other. When one is invited without the other, neither will arrive. Truth without love is a scorching light. Love without truth is a dangerous dream.

The highest understanding is wise love. The greatest love must be for truth. Truth manifests as a common bond of wise love between all creatures. The energy of creation is loving truth -- wise love, the most basic substance, more basic than the atom. To know truth is to know God, the source of love.

The experience of truth alone can foster love, for truth is so all-embracing and integrating that it sees no distinction. Truth is the current and love is the bulb it has to illumine. Through truth, you can experience love; through love, you can visualize truth.

Sathya Sai Speaks 6, p. 190

It is our nature to seek love and truth, for they are springs of our atmic origin. They are the primary sources from which we draw spiritual sustenance. We search for them within and without because we feel our loss without them. We have come from God and ever after seek to return. In the ever-changing world, we catch glimpses and clues to guide us homeward. Piecing together the puzzle, we find that we are ourselves one with God, all love and all truth.

There is in everyone a spark of truth; no one can live without that spark. There is in everyone a flame of love; life becomes a dark void without it. That spark, that flame is God, for he is the source of all truth and all love. Man seeks truth. He seeks to know the reality because his very nature is derived from God, who is truth. He seeks love, to give it and share it, for his nature is of God and God is love.

Sathya Sai Speaks 1, pp. 78-79

Questions for Study Circle

1. Can we only know relative truth, or can we also know absolute truth?

2. Is truth separable from other virtues?

3. Is there a time to speak truth that hurts someone?

4. Is all truth unchanging?

5. Can truth save us in the absence of other virtues?

6. How can we know what is true?

7. How can we practice truth in daily living?

8. How can we know our own truth?

9. What is the relationship between love and truth?

10. What is the source of truth?

11. What is the most essential truth -- the truth of truths?

References for Further Study

1. Sanathana Sarathi, Sept. 1979, pp. 204-205.

2. Sandeha Nivarini, p. 53.

3. Sathya Sai Speaks 4, p. 97 (The king who did not know if dreaming or waking was real).

4. Sathya Sai Speaks 6, p. 189 (Use duty and meditation to discover truth).

5. Sathya Sai Speaks 6, p. 128 (Sai: truth is his name, his message, and his nature).

6. Sathya Sai Speaks 9, pp. 18-20 (The king who would not let truth leave his kingdom).

7. Sathya Sai Speaks 10, pp. 148-149 (Arjuna agrees with Krishna's description of the bird).

8. Sathya Sai Speaks 10, p. 222 (Even if you cannot oblige, speak obligingly).

9. Sathya Sai Speaks 11, p. 203.

10. Summer Showers 1972, pp. 55-56 (The permanent and eternal truth should be one's goal).

11. Summer Showers 1972, pp. 75-76 (The world is neither true nor untrue).

12. Summer Showers 1974, p. 60 (Among all the qualities, truth is the greatest).

13. Summer Showers 1974, p. 71 (Truth has its basis in God).

14. Summer Showers 1977, pp. 206-207.

15. Summer Showers 1978, p. 134.

16. Summer Showers 1978, pp. 184-185 (The king who would not let truth leave his kingdom).

CHAPTER FIFTEEN

Nondualism: Reflections of the Self

1. The Basis of Unity

Unity is one of the most basic principles of spiritual life. There is an innate sense in us that seeks harmony and peace in the midst of the chaos and friction of the world. We naturally search for common elements in all we see. We seek unity far and wide, in the home, the community, the nation, and the world. We strive to find common understanding and universal principles and values. We believe that agreement and brotherhood are our natural states and that enmity comes from misunderstanding. Religion is our exploration of the unity behind diverse appearances.

> *We should recognize that God is present everywhere and that the recognition of the Oneness of God is the basis of all religion.*
>
> *Summer Showers 1978, p. 140*

Yet wherever we search, we often cannot discover the unifying principle. This is because we search for it primarily outside of ourselves. The universal principle is within us; it is our own divine nature, the atma. The divine self is the inmost center from which love emerges to change our world. Divinity in us exists beyond distinctions of sex, color, creed, or nationality. It is the source and the ground of unitive spiritual experience. It is our inner reality and the truth of the external world.

> *Like underground water which is the sustenance of all trees, the atma is the underlying source of all ananda (bliss) that the jivi (individual being) experiences.*
>
> *Sathya Sai Speaks 4, p. 143*

2. Why Does Oneness Appear as Many?

If we place a candle inside a pot with many holes, there appear to be many lights. Although there is just one flame, the pot creates the illusion of many flames. The maya, or illusion of the world, creates the false impression of duality. God is worshiped in many lands by different names, but there is only one all-embracing God. Variations of name and method of worship serve the variety of human attitudes and cultures. Brahman, the universal divine principle, is expressed by individuals and groups according to their understanding, but brahman is one.

So the conception of brahman also will depend on each one's equipment and experience, but that does not mean there are so many different brahmans. A man is called daddy, son, uncle, grandfather, cousin, nephew, and husband -- but that does not make him more than one individual!

Sathya Sai Speaks 3, pp. 108-109

Understanding the unitive principle of nondualism seems at first a formidable task. The path of spiritual understanding from duality to nonduality is a difficult journey. We embark on the adventure believing we are separate and distinct from all others. The beginner does not know where or how to find God, and so he believes God is not present. The very fact of God's omnipresence blinds the aspirant to the reality.

God is everywhere, he is everything, so it appears as if he is nowhere, and he is not in anything! For to know him, you have to identify him as someone foreign and something unique.

Sathya Sai Speaks 7, p. 134

Worldly people believe it necessary to struggle against others to survive in a hostile world. Their egoism causes them to identify with their transitory bodies and personalities. Their attachment to form blinds them to the divinity within. In this state, they have yet to discover immortal atma.

Your own illusion causes you to see the diversity of the world. When we make an attempt to realize and understand the real situation and the nature of the atma, then the diverse names and forms that you see in the world will no longer trouble you. You will be able to fix your attention on the divine aspect, which is one and not many.

Summer Showers 1973, p. 59

Good or bad, beautiful or ugly -- these are our own judgments. God is the creator of it all -- and is all. He manifests through the myriad of opposites. We cannot have day without night; we cannot have the sweet without the bitter. Our task is to accept the manifestations of God's will without passing judgment or questioning his wisdom.

*When divinity is immanent in everything, conscious and
unconscious, in every form of being and becoming, how can
a thing be condemned as bad or commended as good?
Water quenches thirst and drowns people. Fire gives light
and warmth, but also burns and reduces things to ash.
Sound terrifies and also thrills. They are all three divine.
Divinity is inscrutable.*

Sathya Sai Speaks 11, p. 286

As we grow in understanding, we recognize the interdependence of
all people. We cultivate love for family, friends, and community. In the
concluding stages of the transformation, we see that God is within each
person and everything. God is the inner motivator in us, as he is in all
others and all things. Finally, we realize self as a wave upon the ocean,
not different from others or from the ocean of God. The delusion of
separateness, which arises from attachment, is cast off.

*Advaita (nondualism) means all this is atma, then why this
apparent variety? Variety is the picture drawn by the
delusion that you are the body, that you are the "character"
the drama has cast on you!*

Sathya Sai Speaks 4, p. 233

We all climb the spiritual trail toward nondual vision. Jesus at first
described himself as "the messenger of God." Later he described
himself as "the Son of God." Finally his knowledge of unitive
experience led him to declare, "I and my Father are One."

A similar analogy occurs in the Islamic Sufi tradition. First the
pilgrim sees that he is in the light. Next he realizes that the light is in
him. Finally he can say, "I am the light."

3. God: With Form or Without Form?

God is like the wind -- sometimes awe-inspiring, sometimes
soothingly gentle. In snow-swept lands, gusts blow icy cold and
terrifyingly hard. On tropical shores, the breeze is pleasantly warm and
reassuringly gentle. The wind has no form, but we know it according to
its place and time. The warmth or coldness of the wind is dependent on
the quality of its moving air. Its coloration is dependent on dust,
moisture, and sunlight. Similarly, God is without form, but we know
him through his creation. We know of his love and wisdom by seeing
his beauty around us.

As our divine vision grows, we begin to see God in all things. He is the essence of self and everything that exists. The transformation by which we perceive this vision is a function of atma. Through spiritual discipline, we start to disperse the clouds of ignorance. We find unity hidden in diversity. God manifests only by appearance in the world of form. Brahman needs form to manifest and express, just as the wind is inseparable from the air. God is ultimately formless, but we perceive him first through form. Only through shape, color, and size can his sweetness initially be known.

> *This is a silver tumbler. We do not see in this the silver being different from the tumbler. Someone has given me the silver and I have had a tumbler made out of the silver. If the individual asks for his silver back, it is not possible for me to say that he could take the silver and let me retain the tumbler. It is not possible to separate the silver from the tumbler. In this manner, as the silver and the tumbler are inextricably connected with each other, God with form and God without form are connected with each other.*
>
> *Summer Showers 1978, p. 164*

The form and the formless are inseparably linked. For most of us, it is not possible to know God entirely apart from form, nor is it truly possible to experience form apart from God. Whether one worships God by a particular name and form or whether one worships the formless pervasiveness of God, the results of our devotion are the same. God exists in both.

> *The sadhana (spiritual discipline) can be to realize God as formless (nirguna) or with form (saguna). When one walks, the right foot and left foot are both necessary; you cannot hop long on one foot! The saguna sadhana and the nirguna sadhana are as the two feet.*
>
> *Sathya Sai Speaks 6, p. 26*

4. "Atma Is Brahman"

The teaching of nondualism points to an inevitable conclusion: if we know the truth of ourselves, we know the truth of creation. The Upanishads state the important principle, "Atma is brahman." The formless reality of the individual is no different than the reality of the universe.

Einstein theoretically proved that all matter is composed of one finally homogeneous substance, energy. The saints also attest to this unitive principle, but they focus on its essential identity and call it God. When we gain spiritual realization, we know ourselves to be that very principle. We then know ourselves as God, reflected in the world as men and women and children.

> *What is realization? The moment you see your own beauty and are so filled with it that you forget all else, you are free from all bonds; you know that you are all the beauty, all the glory, all the power, all the magnitude of the universe...The reflection of Sivam (God) in the mirror of prakrithi (nature) is jiva (the individual).*
>
> *Sathya Sai Speaks 4, p. 167*

It is difficult to understand how the universe is contained within the individual. However, it is possible to gain the experience of brahman through spiritual discipline. We know all experiences unfold within us. A child's perception of the world is very different from an adult's. But it is not the world that changes; it is our own attitudes and understanding which evolve.

With greater understanding, we realize we are one with all. No dividing line exists between self and other. Where can such a dividing line be found? Does the individual end at the limits of skin, vision, or mind?

> *For ordinary people, it is difficult to understand this infinite nature of divinity. To recognize and understand brahman, we should ourselves be able to experience brahman. One who comprehends brahman becomes identical with brahman.*
>
> *Summer Showers 1977, p. 3*

5. How Can We Understand Nondualism?

If we could in an instant realize that all creation is God, we would cease our search and speculation. The whole of creation is complete and perfect. God encompasses all opposites. Our destiny is to merge with the wholeness of life. We are bound only by the limitations of our experiential knowledge.

As unreal as the limited personality is, bondage is just as unreal. The idea of bondage, like that of liberation, results from the confusion of our minds.

> *The mind of man alone is responsible for both his bondage and his liberation. The difference between bondage and liberation exists only in our thought.*
> *Summer Showers 1974, p. 12*

The perception of bondage is a creation of the ego's manufacture. It is a self-deception of desire and ignorance. In fact, the creation is full and complete when we cease separating it in our minds. To realize this is to experience the truth and bliss of our basic nature. It is our immediate duty and ultimate goal to experience Oneness.

> *So also the universe is but One, though you may be able to distinguish stars and planets, rock and tree, bird and birch, ant and antler in it. Whatever there is, Sarvam Brahmamayam, all is Brahmam. It is all sat-chit-ananda (truth-consciousness-bliss), no more, no less. Realization of this great truth is the only purpose...*
> *Sathya Sai Speaks 7, p. 302*

6. Why Seek the Basis?

We seek the spiritual basis of creation because once it is known, all else is known. It is the key to understanding and inner peace. Without comprehension of Oneness, nothing else can be truly understood. Without understanding, we are held by the spell of maya. Correct action depends on correct knowledge.

The results of pursuing nondualism are found in greater peace and equanimity. When we enlarge our vision to encompass all, we live free from the snares of ego. The worries and frailties which haunt us disappear in unity.

> *When One is realized, there can be no fear, for how can One fear Itself? There can also be no desire, for when there is no second, how can the desire to possess arise? Neither can there be envy, hatred, greed, pride nor any of the evil passions that torment man and allow him no peace. The awareness of One ensures unshaken tranquility, prasanthi.*
> *Sathya Sai Speaks 10, p. 103*

When we accept the divine will as it manifests in this world, we become satisfied with playing our part in the drama. We learn to accept the good and the bad, the beautiful and the ugly. All is the work and wisdom of God. All creatures are manifold aspects of oneself -- the divine. When we achieve this realization, we can live at peace with ourselves and with "others."

One result of this self-realization has been the recognition of everyone else as but the reflection of oneself -- the true basis of unity of mankind.

Sathya Sai Speaks 5, p. 110

Questions for Study Circle

1. Is it possible for us to experience a nondual state?
2. Why does Oneness appear as many?
3. What is the most basic unitive element?
4. If one knows the self, does one also know the reality of all else?
5. Why are there so many religions and so many names for one God?
6. How is unity realized in day-to-day life?
7. Is it possible to realize another's joy or sorrow as our own?
8. Where does "self" end and "other" begin?
9. Is it better to worship God with form or without form?
10. Why should we seek unity?

References for Further Study

1. Gita Vahini, pp. 112-113 (All action is performed by the Lord.)
2. Gita Vahini, pp. 193-194 (God is equally pleased to be worshiped with or without form.)
3. Sathya Sai Speaks 4, p. 233.
4. Sathya Sai Speaks 9, pp. 89-91.
5. Summer Showers 1972, pp. 129-130 (God is in the world like sugar in a glass of water).

6. Summer Showers 1972, p. 130 (One can only talk about nondualism when one has experienced it).

7. Summer Showers 1972, pp. 260-274 (Dualism, qualified nondualism, nondualism).

8. Summer Showers 1973, pp. 245-246.

9. Summer Showers 1974, pp. 48-49 (Why there are so many religions and names of God).

10. Summer Showers 1974, pp. 134-135 (Shankara's nondualism).

11. Summer Showers 1977, pp. 46-55.

12. Summer Showers 1978, pp. 91, 98-101.

13. Summer Showers 1978, pp. 163-164 (Worship of form and formless go together).

14. Summer Showers 1978, p. 173 (Prahlada worshiped formless God).

15. Summer Showers 1979, pp. 99, 102.

16. Summer Showers 1979, p. 157 (All religions lead to God.)

17. Vidya Vahini, p. 61 (The basic truth of creation is unity).

CHAPTER SIXTEEN

Reincarnation: Here We Go Again

1. Evolution of the Soul

The doctrine of reincarnation states that beings live many lives in their quest to reach divinity. Through successive births and deaths even the lowliest creatures evolve into beings of love and wisdom. Through all the stages of evolution, creatures climb the ladder to divinity.

> *Man is a pilgrim set on a long journey: he has started from the stone, moved on to the vegetable and animal, and has now come to the human stage. He has still a long way to go to reach the divine, and so he should not tarry. Every moment is precious; every step must take him further and nearer.*
>
> *Sathya Sai Speaks 8, p. 163*

Through the accumulation of good actions, we have earned human birth. Only through human birth can we consciously reach upward to divinity, and so human birth must be used for the greatest benefit. We must fill our lives with aspiration and good deeds.

> *You have earned this human body by the accumulated merit of many lives as inferior beings, and it is indeed very foolish to fritter away this precious opportunity in activities that are natural only to those inferior beings.*
>
> *Sathya Sai Speaks 5, p. 14*

If we behave in a harmful and low manner, it is possible that we could return to lower levels of evolution. However, it would be unusual to regress so far. The process of development is so slow and steady that such a backward fall would be uncommon.

> *JH (Jack Hislop): Is degrading possible? Is there a rebirth back to the animal?*
>
> *Sai: The possibility is not denied, but it is only rarely that such a thing happens. The degrading of human life due to lack of virtue will normally result in rebirth as a lower grade of human. The total process is always present.*
>
> *My Baba and I, p. 188*

2. Karma, Cause and Consequence

The concept of reincarnation is closely tied to the doctrine of karma. Karma is the law of cause and effect, of spiritual opportunity. Whatever actions we perform have natural consequences. If we do evil actions, we reap evil results. If we perform good actions, we reap good results. The results of actions are not always seen: the consequences may manifest much later. However, results do return at the appropriate time, whether in this lifetime or the next. But all karma provides us with the spiritual opportunities to learn what is required to achieve liberation.

> *You do not see the foundations of a multi-storied skyscraper. Can you, therefore, argue that it simply sits on the ground? The foundations of this life are laid deep in the past, in lives already lived by you. This structure has been shaped by the ground plan of those lives. The unseen decides the bends and the ends: the number of floors, the height, and weight.*

Sathya Sai Speaks 7, p. 46

Divine justice subtly rules our world. We reap the circumstances of our birth and life. The critical events of our lives are not random strokes of fortune or disaster. We earn both our "good" and "bad" circumstances. Through many lifetimes we learn our lessons and evolve toward spiritual maturity.

The process is long, encompassing hundreds or thousands of births. Arjuna, the hero of the Bhagavad Gita, previously lived as a king named Vijaya during the Threta Yuga, a very spiritual era. His ambition was to conquer many kingdoms, a goal not possible in that age of righteousness. To accomplish his goal, he had to be reborn in the following age, when conditions allowed such conquests.[1]

Over the course of many births, each of us also has opportunities to fulfill our desires and thus transcend them. We develop talents and abilities beyond what we could accomplish in one lifetime.

---

1.   *Sathya Sai Speaks 4, pg.145*

What is it that gives each individual this special ability? Is it not what he is carrying with him from his previous birth? You may argue that it is the effort that the individual puts in that is responsible for his becoming either a poet or a singer. This is not the case. You will have to think how, without any special training, these individuals are sometimes exhibiting such special skills.

Summer Showers 1973, p. 37

3. Is the Concept of Reincarnation Something New?

Belief in reincarnation is as old as civilization's earliest memories. The Indian Vedas, as well as the early Greek teachers, were familiar with the doctrine. The concept is central to both Hindu and Buddhist thought. It was also accepted by a considerable body of early Christians and Hasidic Jews. The distinguished third-century Church theologian, Origen (A.D. 185-254), was an early proponent of the teaching. Only in the year 553 A.D. did the Fifth Ecumenical Council, meeting in Constantinople, expunge the doctrine from Church dogma during an unofficial session.[2]

The New Testament contains many references which indicate understanding and belief in reincarnation. Many of the early Jews believed Jesus to be a reincarnation of one of the prophets of the Old Testament. In the New Testament Gospel of Matthew (16:13-14) we read:

When Jesus came into the district of Caesarea Philippi, he asked his disciples, "Who do men say that the Son of man is?" And they said, "Some say John the Baptist, others say Elija, and others Jeremiah or one of the prophets."

Although the teaching is not central to some religious systems, reincarnation forms an esoteric component. The concept is an important foundation of spiritual understanding. In fact, reincarnation and its inseparable relationship to karma is one of the major components of the ageless wisdom, the Sanathana Dharma.

---

2.   *Head & Cranston, Reincarnation in World Thought, pg. 113 (New York: Julain Press, 1967)*

It is only in the Sanathana Dharma that the importance of karma in shaping the destiny of man, the fact of the individual undergoing many births in his progress towards birthlessness, and the mighty grace of God's coming as a man among men to gather them around him in holy companionship for saving them and saving the world through them, is so strongly and clearly laid down. If you doubt any of these great truths, you are certain to suffer and sorrow.

Sathya Sai Speaks 5, pp. 244-245

4. Why Do We Not Remember Past Lives?

Some people do remember past lives. A number of volumes record such experiences.[3] Throughout the world a small but irrefutable number of people have been born with memories of former lifetimes. They have demonstrated knowledge of people and places that they could not have otherwise known.

Sri Sathya Sai Baba relates a wealth of information about his previous incarnation in west central India as Shirdi Sai Baba. He has shown knowledge of that incarnation that he could not have known in any other manner. It is, of course, rare for most people to remember previous lives. The memories of former lifetimes are lost to new experiences and new concerns -- and so God's compassion prevents a probable, overwhelming compounding of our problems.

You know only the present, what is happening before your eyes; you do not know the present is related to the past and is preparing the course for the future. It is like the headlines and titles of a film on the screen: as the letters gleam one after the other, you read them and pass on to the next that comes to view. Each new letter or word wipes out the one already before your eye, just as each birth wipes out the memory of the one already experienced.

Sathya Sai Speaks 3, p. 161

---

3.   *Head & Cranston, Reincarnation in World Thought, Julian Press, 1976 and Ian Stevenson, Twenty Cases Suggestive of Reincarnation, American Society for Psychical Research, 1966.*

The extent of our interest in events also determines how much we remember. We have little cause to remember much of this present life, much less past lives. Our senses and minds are attached to present objects and future ambitions.

> *You may not remember the incidents of a particular day ten years ago, but that does not mean that you were not alive that day. So, too, you may not recall what happened in the previous life or in the life previous to that, but there is no doubt that you had those lives.*
>
> *Sathya Sai Speaks 4, p. 147*

5. Why Escape Rebirth?

Why escape a burning house? We are occupants of a house on fire. The fires of desire, anger, and greed rage throughout our lives. Our lungs fill with the acrid smoke of illusion and ignorance. Like sleepers oblivious to the fire, we do not realize the seriousness of our situation. Only when we reach the safety of the outside can we look back and marvel at our ignorant contentment with that sad state.

Three primary factors result in rebirth: sin, wrong desire, and ignorance. If these are overcome, we can attain release from the cycle of bondage. They are the weights which pull us down into the mire of rebirth.

> *There are three reasons for man to be born. One is sin, the second is an unfulfilled desire for some experience, the third is lack of knowledge, or ignorance. The feeling that he has not fulfilled a desire and his wanting to take birth again to fulfill such a desire is one main reason. Man does several bad things and commits a sin; he has to be reborn to experience the consequences. Ignorance makes you seek a rebirth under these circumstances. These three constitute the basis for our rebirth.*
>
> *Summer Showers 1974, p. 243*

At rebirth we forget all that has happened in past lives. Parents, husbands and wives, children -- all are forgotten. Time and again we eat the same meal of attachment, joy, and grief. After each lifetime it is all lost. All of our cherished possessions go to people we cannot now even remember.

Throughout the dramas of our many lives, only God remains as our closest friend. He watches our progress and patiently waits for us to turn toward him. He watches and provides us with opportunities to develop love and wisdom. He encourages us to cast off desire and attachment to fleeting objects. He alone is our lasting treasure; all other possessions are like the wealth of a dream. We find no true rest until we return to him.

> *Man is on a long pilgrimage towards God. He moves from one life to another to the goal of splendor. On the way he has to take shelter in many caravanserais, or rest houses, but however attractive these may be, he cannot strike root but has to remind himself of the journey's end!*
>
> *Sathya Sai Speaks 6, p. 123*

Our efforts of each lifetime gradually build toward our liberation. No progress is ever lost. It is particularly important for us to advance while circumstances are favorable. A fair wind is used by the wise sailor to full advantage. With the help of the avatar, we may bypass many lifetimes of effort in reaching our goal. If we do not now sail with the fair wind, when will another such opportunity arise?

> *If God, the goal, is not cherished in the memory, one has to wander through many births and arrive home late.*
>
> *Sathya Sai Speaks 3, p. 175*

Questions for Study Circle

1. Why is reincarnation not widely accepted in the West?

2. Why do we not remember past lives?

3. What does reincarnation imply about the way we live?

4. Is it possible for us to know reincarnation as a fact?

5. Why should we believe in reincarnation?

6. Is movement only made upward on the evolutionary ladder?

7. Are the circumstances of our births and lives due to chance?

8. How do we conquer the cycle of births and deaths?

9. Why conquer the birth/death cycle?

2. My Baba And I, p. 188.

3. Sathya Sai Speaks 2, p. 115.

4. Sathya Sai Speaks 4, p. 4.

5. Summer Showers 1973, p. 98 (Wealth in this life is the result of actions in previous lives).

6. Summer Showers 1977, pp. 178-179.

7. Summer Showers 1978, p. 169 (People are reborn as a result of karma).

8. Summer Roses on the Blue Mountains, p. 14 (Rebirth is determined by the manner of death).

CHAPTER SEVENTEEN

Karma: Action and Reaction

1. We Reap What We Sow

Karma is action and the consequence of action. Like a wave, its motion is inseparable from its substance. Physical or mental actions result in consequences directly related to their causes: "As you sow, so shall you reap. " Thus, karma denotes the natural results of action. For example, if a person sows wheat, he should expect to reap wheat at harvest time. Similarly, what we receive in this life is determined by our good or bad actions in past lives -- and, of course, by some of our actions in this lifetime.

> *By doing a bad act, you cannot expect to get a good result, and if you do a good deed, you cannot get a bad reaction from it. The kind of seeds you sow will determine the nature of the crop they will yield.*
>
> *Summer Showers 1977, p. 26*

When we learn a trade or profession, we become qualified to practice that type of work. We learn the skills and develop the necessary experience to perform the work. The cause and effect are obvious. Less obvious is the cause and effect of actions not so closely linked. Good or evil actions may result in unforeseen events long after the original cause is forgotten.

> *We are repaid for our deeds in some way or the other, whether we know it or not, and in the same coin.*
>
> *Summer Showers 1979, p. 10*

The course of our lives is conditioned by the rights we earn and the obligations we incur. So also our physical circumstances and mental and spiritual tendencies are derived from what has gone before. Karma is the spiritual law of justice in action. If karmic law was inoperative, chaos would ultimately result from the disruption of social values. The disruption would be no less than if the physical laws of cause and effect, such as the law of gravity, were removed. Karma is one of the ground rules of the divine game.

Nothing ever happens without proper reason, however accidental or mysterious it might appear. The roots go deep and are out of sight.

Sathya Sai Speaks 7, p. 427

We are not placed randomly in life either to succeed or fail in one lifetime. We live many lives and learn as a result of our experience. The process takes place on a deep level over many lifetimes. Karma is an instrument of this learning process. The tragedies and blessings of life are not dealt with whimsically by God, but are the result of our own actions. We must take responsibility for the course of our own lives.

God is not involved in either rewards or punishment. He only reflects, resounds, and reacts! He is the Eternal Unaffected Witness! You decide your own fate. Do good, be good, you get good in return; be bad, do bad deeds, you reap bad results. Do not thank or blame God. Thank yourself, blame yourself!

Sathya Sai Speaks 7, p. 224

Often we are unaware of the results of our actions. We require time and reflection to realize the consequences of what we do. We may not know the particular error for which we suffer, but we may infer the need to develop more love or consideration for others. The pain spurs us on to find the answer within ourselves.

Of course, when grief overtakes you and pain has you in its grip, the Lord does not always announce the exact sin for which that particular experience is the punishment. You are left to deduce in a general way that every experience is a lesson and every loss is a gain.

Sathya Sai Speaks 2, p. 161

Although we may be unaware of our thoughtlessness, the result still must be experienced. Ignorance is not a release from karma. Escape does not come from denying the validity of the facts.

Whether we do bad work knowingly or unknowingly, the consequences are inevitable. This is the nature of karma.

Summer Showers 1977, p. 157

The results of action cannot be avoided by smart ploys and devious plots. Only by learning and living the lessons taught by the saints and sages can the aspirant be free from the entanglements of karma.

> *You may be very intelligent and clever. All your intelligence and cleverness will not enable you to get over your own karma.*
>
> *Summer Roses on the Blue Mountains, p. 67*

2. How Do We Avoid Bad Karma?

Can we hide in a mountain cave? Can we retreat to a jungle hut? No. The results of wrong action follow closer than our shadow. They adhere to us like tar from the road. Only by walking the path of good actions and scrubbing with the soap of God's grace can we remove that tar.

When we live in accordance with spiritual principles, the negative impact of past karmas dissipates. Although still deep within, the forces lose their power over us. If we live good lives and earn God's grace, the seeds of evil karma are unable to germinate. They do not receive the food and water which enables them to grow. Thus, like a bottle of old medicine, karma is discarded when its shelf life expires.

> *The weight of good acts and thoughts will bury the seeds of bad actions and thoughts. Both good and bad thoughts and impulses are like seeds in the mind. If buried too deeply in the earth, seeds rot and waste away. Good thoughts and deeds bury bad seeds so deeply that they rot and pass away and are no longer ready to spring forth.*
>
> *Conversations, pp. 53-54*

Karma is not a specter which inevitably follows us all the days of our lives. A particular segment of karma may be erased by means of a countering deed. The evil we do may be righted by our performance of good deeds. But just as we may atone for bad deeds with good, we may also lose the fruit of good deeds through bad.

> *The consequence of karma can be wiped out through karma, as a thorn which can be removed only by means of another.*
>
> *Sathya Sai Speaks 4, p. 310*

3. Grace, the Most Effective Antidote

If we are bitten by a poisonous snake, we want an antidote. Once bitten, it is too late to take preventive measures. We need fast relief or we will succumb to the attack. Grace is the antidote for the poisons of the world.

Through divine grace the effects of action may be either totally removed or made painless, though still present. God's grace can overcome any obstacle, however immense. When we earn God's love and grace we may be relieved of a mountain of sin. There is no limit to God's power.

> *You might say that the karma of previous births has to be consumed in this birth and that no amount of grace can save you from that. Evidently, someone has taught you to believe so. But I assure you, you need not suffer from karma like that. When a severe pain torments you, the doctor gives you a morphine injection and you do not feel the pain, though it is still there in the body. Grace is like the morphine; the pain is not felt, though you go through it!...Or the Lord can save a man completely from the consequences, as was done by me for the bhakta whose paralytic stroke and heart attacks I took over some months ago in the Gurupournima week.*
>
> *Sathya Sai Speaks 4, p. 154*

Difficult karma may be removed either by the grace of the Lord or with counteracting karma. But if the lesson of that pain has not been learned, the lesson may have to be repeated. Some people are healed of dreadful diseases by Sai Baba, while others are not.

It may be difficult to understand why. But the Lord sees all the factors involved. He knows who needs to learn the lessons of sickness, and who is ready to be freed from the burden. Events which seem unfortunate are sometimes for our own good. To erase the results of evil action is no favor if we must repeat the lesson. We are fortunate when we are able to meet and overcome past burdens. Each obstacle surmounted brings us nearer to the unitive experience of atma/brahman.

4. The Best Course

We cannot avoid all action, remaining in bed all day for fear of a wrong step. But we can perform our duties without attachment to the results. If we leave the consequences to God, then we are not too concerned with the ups and downs of life. Our duty is to live with love for all. If we act with pure motivations, we can trust in God to watch out for our welfare.

Attachment is a function of the ego. If we act without desire, we avoid treading on the hot coals of karma. But the lessons of action are not always clear. When we seek pleasure, the result is often painful. When we sacrifice our own gain, the result may be sweet. Craving the benefit of action, we become attached to the results. Then our attachment subjects us to pain and loss.

> *If you crave the profit, you will have to be prepared to accept the loss also.*
>
> *Sathya Sai Speaks 4, p. 227*

The solution is not for us to hide in a cave, avoiding even the smallest of actions. It is rather to dedicate our actions to God, acting in a manner consistent with our divine promptings. It is impossible and even undesirable to escape all action. Without action, we could not learn the lessons of this life. Only through action is our character purified and refined.

> *It is not possible for anyone to abstain from action. Action is the basis for our existence. This body has been given to us for the sake of action. It is the need of man's life that he must sanctify it through action and purify his time by right action. This stream of action flows through jnana (wisdom) also and ultimately leads us to the highest stages of realization.*
>
> *Summer Showers 1972, p. 275*

Sathya Sai Baba does not recommend a life away from society for us. He advocates a life of service in the world. Indeed, his own life is an ideal example of such service. Many people are counseled by Sai Baba to marry and raise families. Baba may even offer advice on worldly matters. But our goal must be to act without attachment to the results -- to be "in the world, but not of the world." We should witness the drama of life without becoming ensnared by it.

The art of engaging in karma without getting involved in karma is the thing that has to be learned. Karma has to be done because it is part of one's nature, not out of any external compulsion...So, too, karma done for the profit arising therefrom accumulates consequences which bind a man; it increases in size like a snowball. But karma done without any thought of the fruit therefrom keeps on diminishing and leaves you free from all consequence.

Sathya Sai Speaks 3, p. 96

When we perform our duties well and dedicate them to God, they bring us closer to self-realization. Actions done without desire for rewards promotes equanimity. With equanimity, we free ourselves from pain and loss.

The law of karma holds out hope for you: as the karma, so the consequence. Do not bind yourself further by seeking the fruit of karma. Offer the karma at the feet of God. Let it glorify him, let it further his splendor. Be unconcerned with the success or failure of the endeavor; then death can have no noose to bind you with. Death will come as a liberator, not a jailor.

Sathya Sai Speaks 5, p. 183

When we witness the drama of life yet are not caught by it, we are liberated from desire. We must remember that we are actors in the play of life. It is foolish to be too concerned with the fate of actors playing a role.

Do all karma as actors in a play, keeping your identity separate and not attaching yourself too much to your role. Remember that the whole thing is just a play and the Lord has assigned you a part. Act your part well: there all your duty ends.

Sathya Sai Speaks 1, p. 172

5. Karma Saves the Kitten

Karma is a two-sided sword. We fear the results of our bad actions, but only through karma can we gain spiritual freedom. It is wise to regard karma as an ally. We must befriend karma through action free from attachment; then it aids us in our battle.

> *Karma can save as well as kill. It is like the cat that bites: it bites the kitten in order to carry it in its mouth to a place of safety; it bites the rat in order to kill and eat. Become the kitten and karma will rescue you like a loving mother. Become a rat and you are lost.*
>
> *Sathya Sai Speaks 1, p. 13*

Bliss is derived from living with spiritual discrimination and detachment. Without wrong desire and ensnaring attachment, life yields happiness. Bliss may be experienced both in the journey and at the destination.

> *There is more joy in the doing of karma than in the fruit it may give. The pilgrimage is often more pleasurable than the actual experience of the temple to which the pilgrim went.*
>
> *Sathya Sai Speaks 1, pp. 178-179*

Karma is the medicine for overcoming bondage to the cycle of birth and death. Wisdom is earned through karma. Through this human birth, we rise to liberation. The play of cause and effect teaches us the essential lessons which enable us to attain spiritual freedom.

> *It is only through karma that devotion can be deepened. Karma cleanses the mind and makes it fit for jnana."*
>
> *Sathya Sai Speaks 4, pp. 83-84*

The process of living and learning through the lessons of karma ultimately brings us to liberation. If we do not live and learn, how will we ever know ultimate truth?

> *Only through karma can liberation be effected...Without karma, progress is very difficult.*
>
> *Sathya Sai Speaks 4, p. 124*

Questions for Study Circle

1. What is karma?

2. What is the relationship of karma and reincarnation?

3. Is karma good or bad in its effects on us?

4. Are the events of our lives predestined, do we have free will, or is there a mixture of both?

5. How can we overcome the effects of karma?

6. How can we avoid the consequences of karma?

7. Can grace overcome karma?

8. How can we act without attachment to results?

9. Do thoughts create karma?

10. If karma and reincarnation did not exist, would you consider this a just world with a loving God?

References for Further Study

1. Bhagavad Gita, chapter 3.

2. Conversations, p. 111 (Past, present, and future karma).

3. Dhyana Vahini, pp. 1-2.

4. Gita Vahini, pp. 47-48 (Everyone must engage in karma).

5. Gita Vahini, pp. 134-135 (Primal karma).

6. Gita Vahini, pp. 247-250 (Nishkama karma).

7. Gita Vahini, p. 265 (Dushkarma, sath-karma, misra-karma, jnana-karma).

8. Sathya Sai Speaks 2, pp. 114-116.

9. Sathya Sai Speaks 4, p. 168 (You create your own karma).

10. Sathya Sai Speaks 6, p. 111.

11. Sathya Sai Speaks 11, pp. 157-159 (Types of karma).

12. Summer Showers 1972, pp. 154-156 (Prarabhda, sanchita, and agami karma).

13. Summer Showers 1972, p. 276 (Karma, vikarma, akarma).

14. Summer Showers 1974, p. 223 (What is karma?).

15. Summer Showers 1977, pp. 26-29.

16. Summer Showers 1979, pp. 4-6, 10 (Nishkama karma).

17. Summer Showers 1979, pp. 108-109.

18. Summer Roses on the Blue Mountains, p. 106 (On the path of karma yoga the aspirant relies on personal strength).

CHAPTER EIGHTEEN

The Atma: Our Divine Nature

1. Know Thyself

Humanity has from the earliest days tried to understand its own nature. We have turned in every direction to find our place under the stars. From earliest times, people worshiped their ancestors and nature. They created pantheons of gods and goddesses to personify divine traits. They developed systems of philosophy, psychology, and religion.

There is no end to the ways in which human beings have sought their identity and life's meaning, but the ultimate answer has eluded most of us. We have sought outwardly for a goal which lies inside us. When we search within, we have a chance for far greater success.

> *There cannot be anything more useful than knowledge of one's own self. What do we mean by knowledge about one's own self? It is the knowledge of the atma (inner divinity). To know the atma and to know one's own self is the most useful aspect of one's learning.*
>
> *Summer Showers 1977, p. 46*

It is said that in the earliest days the gods wished to hide our divinity from us. The gods considered as hiding places the highest mountain peaks and the deepest ocean canyons. They finally decided that the last place human beings would search would be in their own hearts.

Rarely do people look deeply within themselves, but when they have, great saints and sages have emerged. A saint of India, Ramana Maharshi, recommended that his disciples ask continually, "Who am I?" Through deep introspection, the answer inevitably emerges: "I am divinity itself." Jesus Christ said to his followers, "The kingdom of heaven is within you." (Luke 17:20-21.) Atma, not the personality, holds the secret of our blissful fulfillment.

Your reality is the atma, a wave of the paramatma (universal divinity). The one object of this human existence is to visualize that reality, that atma, that relationship between the wave and the sea. All other activities are trivial; you share them with birds and beasts. But this is the unique privilege of man. He has clambered through all the steps of the ladder of evolution in order to inherit this high destiny.

Sathya Sai Speaks 6, p. 224

2. Atma, the God Within

The traditions of self-realization are not unknown to Western religion. Witness the teachings, for example, of St. Ignatius Loyola (the so-called classic method of meditation), the Orthodox Churches (the Prayer of the Heart, a method of repeating the name of the Lord), the Sulpician Oratorian Fathers (the "head" and "heart" meditation), Martin Luther (structured meditation, but to be abandoned in the Presence of the Holy Spirit), the Kabbala, the Quakers (hearkening to the "inner voice"), and especially, perhaps, Meister Eckhart, the German mystic, and Jan van Ruysbroeck, the Flemish mystical theologian.

However, the systematic understanding of the divine journey has been more notable in the Eastern disciplines. For thousands of years, a great spiritual tradition has flourished in India. The ancient teachings of realized sages have been passed from teacher to student. The Vedas, particularly the Upanishads, contain the teachings necessary for self-transformation. They illuminate the message of the divine self, the atma, characterized by being, consciousness, and bliss. The atma resides in all of us as our guide and goal -- the identity sought in the question, "Who am I?"

The atma is immanent in everyone. It is the spark of divinity which gives him light, love, and joy.

Sathya Sai Speaks 9, p. 15

Because divinity is inherent in all, we all have an opportunity for God-realization. Realization can be achieved by the beggar or the king, the educated person or the illiterate. It is not dependent on sex, age, or status, only on the spiritual consciousness of the seeker. The goal is the same for all. All are finally driven to achieve that victory by the growing experiential knowledge of who and what we most essentially are.

There may be differences among men in physical strength, financial status, intellectual acumen, but all are equal in the eyes of God; all have the right and the potentiality to achieve the goal of merging in him. Note that everyone, from the beggar to the billionaire, is prompted by the urge to achieve ananda, supreme bliss, based on inner peace, unaffected by ups and downs. Every activity, however elementary or earth-shaking, is subservient to this ideal.

Sathya Sai Speaks 8, p. 77

Due to our own misunderstanding, some people fear the loss of individuality that liberation seems to imply. However, the truth is that we are not the small body or personality with which we identify. We are greater and more complete than the wave: we are the ocean.

A story is told about the king of the gods, Indra. He once had to take birth as a pig, resulting from the curse of a great holy man. After some time, Indra forgot that he was king of the gods. He wallowed in the mud of his yard and took on the cares of an ordinary hog. His only concern was for his piglets, his sow, and his feed trough.

When the other gods came to wake him from his pitiable state, he cried in grief. He did not want to be removed from his sty and his porcine family. He had forgotten his blissful divine nature. But upon awaking from that life he realized his error. Similarly, we have forgotten our divine nature and become attached to the petty pleasures and griefs of our small concerns.

But please do not be afraid of reaching the goal of moksha (liberation)! Do not conceive that stage as a calamity. It is the birth of joy, a joy that knows no decline, and the death of grief, grief that will never more be born.

Sathya Sai Speaks 3, p. 178

3. The Source Of Understanding

The Rosetta Stone unlocked the mystery of Egyptian hieroglyphics. That slab of black basalt, found in 1799, held the key to the ancient codes. That single tablet enabled Egyptologists to use a known language on the stone to decipher the meanings of countless ancient Egyptian inscriptions. However, even that black basalt pales beside a greater key: the Atmic experience of self-realization, which enables us to know our identity and the purpose of our life. It is the light that illumines the immortal truth of our divine state. The atma is the light that penetrates our fog of illusion to reveal our divinity.

When the atma is understood, everything else is understood. All effects are subsumed by the cause.

Upanishad Vahini, p. 39

It is quite possible to attain the Atmic vision while still in the body. There need not be a long-term loss of relative, everyday identity and role -- but these do disappear in the experience of Oneness. While functioning as a person, then, we have the potential for realizing our nature as divine. Many spiritual masters and advanced disciples have achieved this blissful state and have continued their missions for many years. When the experience of Oneness is attained, the goal is won. There are no prerequisites of superior intellect or graying hair.

When the obstacles in the path of truth are laid low, deliverance is achieved. That is why moksha is something that can be won here and now; one need not wait for the dissolution of the physical body for that.

Sathya Sai Speaks 3, p. 140

The truth is known when we explore our own consciousness. The path is inward. To understand God, we need only to understand ourselves.

When you cannot reach down to your own basic reality, why waste time in exploring the essence of Godhead? As a matter of fact, you can understand me only when you have understood yourself, your own basic truth.

Sathya Sai Speaks 2, p. 141

When we experience our divinity, we find we were never bound. Bondage, like liberation, lies in our minds. We bind ourselves with the ropes of attachment and wrong desire. Like Indra in the pig form, we are caught by our own ignorance of our self-nature. We must cast off desires and wrong thoughts and allow our souls to rise to their divine destiny.

The Gita directs that even the eagerness to be liberated is a bond. One is fundamentally free; bondage is only an illusion. So the desire to unloosen the bond is the result of ignorance.

Sathya Sai Speaks 10, p. 246

Self-fulfillment is a state of true independence. We can know complete contentment and joy whatever external circumstances we face. Liberation is the process of fully coming to terms with ourself, without any semblance of bondage. It is the process of reconciling all internal contradictions -- stilling the mind and experiencing essential being, consciousness, and bliss (sat-chit-ananda).

> *Moksha is only another word for independence -- not depending on any outside thing or person.*
>
> *Jnana Vahini, p. 6*

When we realize our innermost being as divinity, we also recognize others as divine. The waves of the ocean are not separate from each other, nor from the whole, which is God. When we perceive God within ourselves, we also see God within all others.

> *All is divine. When you are firmly established in the fact of your divinity, then you will directly know that others are divine.*
>
> *Conversations, pp. 115-116*

If we are joyful embodiments of Oneness, why do we not feel that way? It is because we obscure the ever-present sun of God with the black clouds of selfish egoism. We cling to our limited personalities and hide our light. Our imaginations create fears, cravings, death, and all manner of limitations. As a result of improper training, we distort the clear and pure vision of divinity.

4. Realize Yourself and Be Free

When we awaken from a dreadful nightmare, we are greatly relieved. The terrifying monsters of the night evaporate with the dawn. All the horror is seen to be our own creation, projected by our mind. But another step must still be taken, for we must now awaken from our waking dream. Fears and monsters of a more subtle nature continue to pursue us because we still fail to see the reality of omnipresent God.

Spiritual practice enables us to assert our true nature, the universal self. We learn to see through the illusion of the body and realize that we are, in fact, the totality of our consciousness. We grow in love and wisdom beyond what we thought possible. Until this state of blissful joy is attained, we feel that something is missing. We continue to strive until we know our true nature.

Do not tell me that you do not care for that bliss, that you are satisfied with the delusion and are not willing to undergo the rigors of sleeplessness. Your basic nature, believe me, abhors this dull, dreary routine of eating, drinking, and sleeping. It seeks something it knows it has lost -- santhi, inward contentment. It seeks liberation from bondage to the trivial and temporary. Everyone craves for it in his heart of hearts. And it is available only in one shop -- contemplation of the highest self, the basis of all this appearance.

Sathya Sai Speaks 1, p. 115

There is no limit to the eternal truth of a human being. The boundaries between self and others are false limitations. Where do the limitations exist? Are we limited by our physical bodies, by our range of sight, or even by our minds? No. The limitations are self-imposed by the wrong desires and wrong thoughts of our egoism.

You and the Universal are One; you and the Absolute are One; you and the Eternal are One. You are not the individual, the particular, the temporary. Feel this. Know this. Act in conformity with this.

Sathya Sai Speaks 4, p. 236

To enlarge our vision to encompass all within ourselves, we must cultivate selfless love. Love shelters all within its fold. The mind separates, the heart unifies. Love is the method to realize the divine. When we feel another's joy and sorrow as our own, we may be confident of our progress on the path. God is the ocean of love into which all of us must plunge. Love is the royal road for realization of the goal.

Realization, which is not possible through logic, which is not possible through offering sacrifices, and which is not possible through discussion and other disciplines, can be achieved only through love.

Summer Showers 1972, p. 249

Questions for Study Circle

1. What is the atma?

2. How do we discover our true nature?

3. What do others tell us about ourselves?

4. Is there anything to fear in liberation?

5. How is liberation achieved?

6. Why is the concept of spiritual liberation uncommon in the West?

7. What are the characteristics of the liberated person?

8. Is the atma the key to all understanding?

9. Do we all have an identical divine nature?

10. How do we give up the desire for liberation and still attain it?

11. How do the scriptures and the saints describe our essential nature?

References for Further Study

1. Conversations, p. 102 (The distinction between divine vision and God-realization).

2. Dhyana Vahini, p. 59 (Both good and bad must be overcome for liberation).

3. Jnana Vahini, p. 64 (Desire for liberation is the result of good past karma).

4. Sathya Sai Speaks 1, p. 192 (The truth of all is the same).

5. Sathya Sai Speaks 3, p. 183.

6. Sathya Sai Speaks 10, pp. 263-266.

7. Sathya Sai Speaks 11, p. 216 (atma).

8. Summer Showers 1973, p. 128 (The goal of life is to realize the atma).

9. Summer Showers 1974, pp. 33-42 (Brahman).

10. Summer Showers 1974, pp. 202-203 (The divine self is hidden by clouds of ego).

11. Summer Showers 1977, pp. 28-29 (Liberation comes when the mind is free of desire).

12. Summer Showers 1977, pp. 46-51, 56, 66, 75-79 (The nature of atma).

13. Summer Showers 1979, p. 13 (Spiritual beatitude is gained by grace).

14. Upanishad Vahini, pp. 49-50 (Atma has no limitation, attribute, or quality).

15. Upanishad Vahini, p. 51 (Atma flashes like a stream of lightning).

Part Three: Practicing Love

CHAPTER NINETEEN

Love: The Royal Road

1. The Basis of Creation

If a reason could be given for the purpose of creation, it could be stated most simply as "love." For the Lord to create the cosmos from the void of pre-time, there must have been a motive of special significance. Surely just the manifestation of material and technological marvels was not enough; the creation of men and nations was not enough. There must have been an element which would justify and fulfill the creation.

Love was the reason and continues to be the justification. It is the attraction principle of divinity, wherein all creatures find their common origin and bond. Love is the energy of creation, which manifests as positive and negative currents. In the polarity of opposites, all creation came into being and forever afterward seeks its union. In the return journey to union with spirit, the material form is purified and transformed into divine love and selflessness.

> *The basis for the entire world is the prema (divine love) of the Lord. Even if one is able to get by heart the essence of all the Vedas (sacred teachings) and even if one is able to compose poetry in a very attractive manner, if that person does not have a purified heart, he is a useless person. What other greater truth can I communicate to you?*
> *Summer Roses on the Blue Mountains 1976, p. 99*

The world is the field in which love grows and is harvested. It is a battlefield of the senses, where the play of good and evil is acted out. Love vies against the selfish desires of the ego. The reality of unity struggles to overcome the illusion of separateness. The experience of selfless love reveals God in the individual and within all creatures.

Love is the word which indicates the striving to realise the falsehood of the many and the reality of the One. Love identifies; hate separates. Love transposes the self on to another and the two think, speak, and act as one. When love takes in more and more within its fold, more and more entities are rendered as One. When you love me, you love all, for you begin to feel and know and experience that I am in all.

Sathya Sai Speaks 7, p. 473

Unitive love is the fulfillment of life. It expresses itself as identification with all, for as we grow in spiritual awareness, we expand the bounds of our compassion. We start by loving ourselves, then our family, community, and nation. However, true love is gained only when we see through all false distinctions. When we see God in all creation, we cease to selectively love only some and not others. This awareness fulfills life's promise.

The Earth is a great enterprise, a busy factory, where the product is love. By means of sadhana (spiritual practice), it is posssible to produce love and export it to millions and millions of people in need of it. The more it is shared, the deeper it becomes, the sweeter its taste, and the vaster the joy. By means of love, one can approach God and stay in his presence, for God is love, and when one lives in love he is living in God.

Sathya Sai Speaks 7, p. 395

2. How Do We Cultivate Love?

To grow flowers, we must first clear a plot of ground. To grow love, we must clear the weeds of attachment and greed from our hearts. Soil must be watered and fertilized. The heart must be prepared by learning compassion for all. When the tender shoots of service and devotion sprout, they must be kept free of the insects of egoism.

We start by expressing love toward God as we would to a mother or father, brother or sister. But with time we see that there is no limit to the attributes and manifestations of God. The world is created from and is the substance of God. And so we begin to recognize God in all and express love as service and sympathy for those in need. With time, we feel the joys and sorrows of others as our own. By serving others, we revere God within them and draw closer to the source.

*Love is God, God is love. Where there is love, there God is
certainly evident. Love more and more people, love them
more and more intensely. Transform the love into service,
transform the service into worship. That is the highest
sadhana.*

Sathya Sai Speaks 4, p. 309

Service is the natural expression of love in action. When our hearts
are distressed at the suffering of others, we have no choice but to
alleviate that suffering. That is the true test of love. Service is rendered
as to a friend, not as a duty. Service is performed as a token of love and
humility, gladly given.

Love is not an obligation; it is an expression of our inner divinity.
Service should not be performed with the idea of one serving and
another being served. Selfless service is a natural expression of love,
given joyfully and spontaneously. Love is our nature; it is the fountain
of divinity, our inner source, identity, and potential.

*When you live with the consciousness of the omnipresent
atma (inner divinity), you live in love, love flowing and
flooding in and through you and all else.*

Sathya Sai Speaks 7, p. 25

To experience the flood of love requires spiritual practice. It is
acquired by purification of character. The prerequisites to experience
divine love are truthfulness, nonviolence, inner peace, and adherence
to duty. When we live a virtuous and moral life, we can experience
selfless love.

*If we really want to experience prema, we will have to
understand what peace, or shanti, means. If we want to
follow the path of peace, we will have to accept the path of
dharma (spiritual duty). If we want to follow the path of
dharma, we will have to accept the path of truth.*

Summer Showers 1977, p. 60

3. The Vision of Unity

Saintly men and women reach beyond their own small worlds to
grasp universal values. They seek higher and further for the principles
which benefit all. Their visions for humanity germinate in hearts full of
love. Their ideals are nurtured on the milk of truth and the bread of duty.

They grow strong in the shelter of inner peace. Their strength is inner divinity realized through a pure heart.

The pinnacle of spiritual attainment is realization of the atma. The qualities of this divine nature are being-consciousness-bliss, experienced with divine love as truth. At the summit of realization, these qualities meet at a common point, which is beyond description. So to reach the height of love, one must also reach the apex of wisdom, sense of duty, and peace. These qualities are present within each of us, but are hidden by the dark clouds of egoism. Sathya Sai Baba says that these divine qualities are like the sun: they always shine within us, but are often hidden by clouds of selfishness.

> *The Upanishads say that man is a spark of divine love encased in five sheaths...That love is ever urging and surging for expression, enlargement, and enclasping. But the tangles of fear, greed, egoism, and aggrandizement do not allow the spark to grow and illumine the sheaths, as well as the world around.*
>
> *Sathya Sai Speaks 7, p. 324*

When we foster divine love within, the dark clouds disperse. Through love, self-realization is achieved. When we love God, we will not do anything to remove ourselves from the source of love. God wields the instrument of love to transform and reform us into the image of the divine.

> *One should not fear God. One must love him so much that all acts he disapproves are discarded. Fear to do wrong; fear to hate another; fear losing grace.*
>
> *Sathya Sai Speaks 6, p. 179*

4. God Is Won by Love

In all the world's religions, we find no saints who attained God by means of their scholarship; we find no saints who realized the Lord by means of good deeds alone. Love is the price for admission to God's presence. If we have love in abundance, no other requirement is needed. Love unites the individual with divinity. Through love, we gain nearness to God. Wisdom or austerities alone cannot enable us to achieve realization of our goal.

Cultivate love and prema towards all: that is the way to gain nearness. I do not measure distance in terms of meters or miles. The range of love decides distance for me.
                                                    Sathya Sai Speaks 6, p. 263

Love reveals and is the presence of God. Love is the light by which his face is lit. If we wish to know and experience God, we must learn love for God's creatures. We cannot express devotion to God without also loving his creation. When we experience the source of love within, we view the world through the glasses of love.

I must tell you of the paramount importance of love. Love is God; live in love. God is the embodiment of perfect love. He can be known and realized, reached and won, only through love. You can see the moon only with the help of moonlight; you can see God only through the rays of love.
                                                    Sathya Sai Speaks 8, pp. 181-182

Sathya Sai Baba teaches us a short prescription that enables us to reach the goal.

Start the day with love

Spend the day with love

Fill the day with love

End the day with love

That is the way to God

                                                    Sathya Sai Speaks 8, p. 73

Questions for Study Circle

1. What is love?

2. How is love cultivated?

3. Why develop love?

4. How is love expressed?

5. What is the true test of love?

6. Is love emotional or unreasonable?

7. Can love exist without being expressed?

8. Can God be known without cultivating love?

9. What is so special about love?

10. Can we love God without loving other people?

11. Where does love come from?

References for Further Study

1. Bhagavad Gita, Chapter 12.

2. Sathya Sai Speaks 1, p. 43 (The Lord is reflected in the heart with love).

3. Sathya Sai Speaks 6, p. 86 (Love is the distinguishing mark of Sai).

4. Sathya Sai Speaks 6, p. 225 (The atma expresses itself as love).

5. Sathya Sai Speaks 9, p. 107 (God is bound to you by love).

6. Sathya Sai Speaks 11, p. 99 (The glasses of love make everything appear as love).

7. Sathya Sai Speaks 11, p. 239 (To experience love you must throw away desire).

8. Summer Showers 1974, p. 107 (If one has on the glasses of love, all appears as love).

9. Summer Showers 1976, pp. 106-111.

10. Summer Roses on the Blue Mountains, p. 107 (Love is the only way to reach and understand God).

CHAPTER TWENTY

Song: Language of the Soul

1. Inspiration for the Journey

Song is a tonic for the weary; it lightens our souls and fills us with the taste of heaven. Spiritual music is a universal language of the heart.

Devotional singing occupies a prominent role in almost every religious tradition. Whether in hymns, chants, choral music, or bhajans, the intent of devotional song is to uplift the spirit and affirm divine glory. The group activity promotes faith and confers joy. Through group singing, we gain spiritual confidence and receive encouragement to progress on the Godward path. Singing is an exercise with potentially important results.

> *Bhajan (devotional song) is one of the processes by which you can train the mind to expand into eternal values. Teach the mind to revel in the glory and majesty of God. Wean it away from petty horizons of pleasure...Bhajan induces in you a desire to experience the truth, to glimpse the beauty that is God, to taste the bliss that is the Self. It encourages man to dive into himself and be genuinely his real Self.*
> *Sathya Sai Speaks 7, pp. 468-469*

By participating in song meetings, we derive many benefits. Love and devotion well up in our hearts. Remembrance of God becomes constant and steady. The practice speeds us on the path to winning the Lord's grace. With effort and devotion, God's blessings are won.

> *The tongue is a post, bhajan is the rope; with that rope, you can bring God Almighty near you and tie him up so that his grace becomes yours. God is so kind that he will yield to your prayers and get bound. You have only to call on him to be by your side, with you, leading you and guiding you.*
> *Sathya Sai Speaks 7, p. 52*

When we sing with devotion, joy is likely to remain in our hearts all day long. Song becomes a source of inspiration and consolation that transforms our lives. The effort results in expanded consciousness of the presence of God. That awareness promotes faith and peace.

You must pass your days in song. Let your whole life be a bhajan. Believe that God is everywhere at all times and derive strength, comfort, and joy, singing in your heart in his presence the glory of God. Let melody and harmony surge up from your hearts and let all take delight in the love that you express through that song.

Sathya Sai Speaks 10, p. 75

The joy which we derive from song helps to sustain and encourage us on the path. It binds us to the Lord and attracts his grace. God derives joy from our joy. When we draw closer to him, the Lord draws closer to us. The bliss of song binds us to him as few other practices can.

The ananda (bliss) that I derive from bhajan I do not get from anything else.

Sathya Sai Speaks 8, p. 48

2. The Song Meeting

To get at the sweet juice of a coconut, we must first peel off the fibrous husk and crack the hard nut. In the same manner, to enjoy devotional songs, some preparatory tasks must be accomplished. For the song meeting to be harmonious and beneficial, proper guidelines have to be adopted. Clear organization and policies help to eliminate misunderstandings.

When one member is placed in charge of the activity, there is less chance for confusion. This allows for the orderly development of the session. As the number of members grows, changes have to be made. Suggestions need to be monitored and implemented by a knowledgeable individual or committee.

The decoration of the hall and arrangement of the session should not suggest pomp and undue expense. It is best kept simple and devotional. Ideally the session is convened in a clean and accessible location. All participants should feel welcome to attend. Song meetings should spread good will and tolerance in the community.

Bhajan must spread good will, love, ecstasy. It must invite all to share in the joy and peace.

Sathya Sai Speaks 8, p. 47

To foster an atmosphere of peace and love, it is beneficial to start the meeting with omkar (the repetition of Om) and to conclude with a short meditation.[1] This establishes a feeling of brotherhood and cooperation among all.

The group must also decide what its objectives will be. For example, a song center may decide to encourage young members to participate in singing and leading songs. Members may decide that the participation of young members is more important than maintaining high musical standards. This is particularly true when young members are inexperienced at leading songs or playing instruments. The price must be evaluated by the participants in light of the benefits.

Another policy which should be discussed at the outset is song selection, particularly language preferences. It is desirable for the group to sing in the language of their country of residence. Of course, some variety should be encouraged, but it is important that our meetings appeal to newcomers from the community around us. We must help more and more people to know the great love of Sai. It is usually easier for participants to experience the devotion of a song when they understand and can pronounce the words.

3. Standards: Musical or Devotional?

Devotion is the stamp which posts our loving thoughts to God. A mother cares more for the scrawl of her children than for the beautiful script of a stranger; God listens to our hearts more than to our words.

It is not the perfection of musical talent alone which pleases the Lord. Devotion and sincerity should also be expressed. It is good to encourage wholehearted participation and enthusiasm. Where is the benefit if we are timid and do not sing out?

> *Some do not sing loud at bhajans. When a man has fallen into a well and is unable to get out, does he mutter to himself? Clap your hands with vigor so that the birds of evil and passion infesting your minds shall fly away.*
> *Sanathana Sarathi, Dec. 1980, p. 256*

It is also desirable, however, that tunes be sung in a harmonious and pleasing manner. Musical training or the learning of scales is not required. What is required is that our singing be a natural reflection of

---

1.   *Sathya Sai Speaks 6, pg. 221*

our yearning for God. When we sing with devotion, our joy naturally sweetens the melody.

> *Bhajan must be a felt experience. Do not sing with one eye on the effect the song makes on the listeners and the other on the effect it makes on God. Let your heart pant for God; then raga and tala will automatically be pleasant and correct.*
>
> *Sathya Sai Speaks 8, p. 60*

At a public meeting, it may be necessary for some individuals to express their enthusiasm silently. Praises sung in a discordant manner do little to elevate our spirits. Standards must be met for the musical quality of a public session.

> *Let those with a good voice and musical talent lead. The keertan (song) must be pleasant; it should not jar on the ear. If your voice is grating or out of tune, do not disturb the melody, but repeat the Namavali (the name of the Lord in song) in your mind.*
>
> *Sathya Sai Speaks 7, p. 172*

Another difficulty may arise when working with the most musically talented members. These members may wish to widen the scope of compositions to be sung. In seeking new songs and some variety, they may select songs which are too difficult for other members to follow. There may even be a tendency for some leaders to compete in musical virtuosity. They may display their egos more than devotion, an occurrence directly contrary to the purpose of the discipline.

> *I do not like bhajan that promotes rivalry or envy or egoism or that emanates from intolerance.*
>
> *Sathya Sai Speaks 6, p. 266*

Variety in the program is desirable. New songs help to build our interest and enthusiasm. One effective way to do this is to schedule regular learning sessions. In these sessions, leaders and members can improve their skills and learn new songs. It may be necessary to require leaders to attend these sessions so they can determine if they are prepared to sing the new composition.

4. Take Up the Practice

Song is a key which sometimes can unlock even the hardest hearts. It is like the sun that carries even the heaviest clouds across the sky: their leaden mass is lifted by the divine warmth.

So all should take up the practice of singing to the Lord. Excuses should not be found for missing the song meeting. Each of us has a contribution to make -- if only by appreciative listening. Our discipline of regular practice needs to be steadily maintained. For this reason, Sathya Sai Baba recommends regular attendance.

> *Attend all the sessions in the hall...Do not take shelter behind excuses. If you are ill, bhajan will help the cure, or, let me tell you, it is far better to die during the bhajan with the Lord's name on the lips.*
>
> *Sathya Sai Speaks 2, p. 186*

Harmony and devotion must ultimately be the result of a good song meeting. All who participate must work together with tolerance and the knowledge that the Lord himself is present. When this is done, each of us feels the divine bliss burn brighter within our hearts and we experience the presence of our Lord.

> *Wherever my bhakta sings my name, I am present there.*
>
> *Sanathana Sarathi, June 1984, p. 161*

Questions for Study Circle

1. How do devotional songs assist our spiritual growth?

2. What are the essential ingredients of spiritual songs?

3. Who is qualified to lead songs?

4. What place do children have at song meetings?

5. Should songs be sung in any one particular language?

6. Are some names better to sing than others?

7. Who maintains proper standards, and how?

8. How often should devotional sessions be held?

9. Where should meetings be convened?

References for Further Study

1. Sathya Sai Speaks 6, p. 220 (Hold bhajans where all will be welcomed).

2. Sathya Sai Speaks 7, p. 411 (Sing a variety of names, with each line only repeated twice).

3. Sathya Sai Speaks 9, p. 162 (When you sing for joy, then only can you confer joy on others).

4. Sathya Sai Speaks 9, pp. 161-162 (There should be no factionalism at bhajans).

CHAPTER TWENTY- ONE

Miracles: Outward Signs of Inner Events

1. What Is a Miracle?

A miracle is an event that does not appear to be the result of any known natural law or agency. A miracle is also commonly defined as a wonderful or amazing thing, fact, or event. The miracles of Sai Baba fit both definitions.

Many have read or heard about the Sai miracles. Some devotees have experienced miracles themselves. Perceptions vary widely among newcomers on the usefulness and validity of these happenings. It would be an error to place too much emphasis on these events. However, the stories are often told because they can easily be related, and it is possible to quickly capture the interest of another person in relating these experiences. It is not so easy to express the unbounded love of Sai in a short narration.

Much depends on what one considers to be a miracle. An event which one observer considers to be a great mystery may be easily explained by another. The observer's background and experience are often the deciding factors. A miraculous event may strongly impact one person, while causing little or no effect on another. In judging the value of these signs, we must consider the purpose and results.

2. Why Do Some People Believe and Others Do Not?

If we believe in the appearance of miracles, we must have some faith in the agency that causes them. That faith is a foundation which is built slowly with a sincere and open mind, experience, and understanding of divine principles. To benefit from miracles, we must be willing to examine them and analyze their implications for us. Many people will ignore such signs as inexplicable or without bearing on their own situation.

Historical miracles are less difficult for us to accept than present-day miracles. It is not difficult for us to believe that Jesus manifested miracles two thousand years ago, but it is difficult for us to think that similar events are happening now. History demands less of us than our own experience, for our experience requires us to consider the implications to the way we live.

> You believe in such things when they are related of Rama or Krishna or others, for you feel that belief does not impose any obligations on you. But in the case of the incarnation before you, you apprehend that when the divine is recognized, certain consequences follow, and you try to avoid them.
>
> *Sathya Sai Speaks 7, p. 381*

When we accept the validity of modern-day miracles, we are obligated to account for what we have seen. It is not difficult to ignore history, but it is difficult for us to discount our own experience. Experiencing a higher power or spiritual cause in our own life morally obligates us to live a more responsible life.

For this reason, we may be selective in the miracles we choose to recognize. The "miracles" of television or space travel require little of us, but a miracle performed by a spiritual teacher requires some thought and introspection. Depending on how willing we are to investigate these occurrences, a miracle may have great effect on one person and no effect on another.

Miracles often seem to be outward signs of inner happenings. A miraculous event carries little meaning if we have not previously done the work which makes us receptive to the message. A miracle is a seed which can grow into a flower of love and truth. However, for the seed to grow, proper preparation of the soil must first be accomplished. This requires ongoing effort. Even then, unless the recipient is deserving and the circumstance is exceptional, a miraculous event may not occur.

> An Avatar is capable of all things at all times, yet the Avatar will not undertake to demonstrate his powers at all times. An Avatar will undertake to demonstrate such powers when exceptional circumstances demand it and will shed the grace on a deserving person only.
>
> *Summer Roses on the Blue Mountains, p. 51*

3. Why Does Sai Baba Perform Miracles?

Sai Baba's miracles shake us from complacency. They reveal his personal love, omniscience, and attention to us. Wonderful signs announce Baba's divine nature and mission. But the miracles are only granted to those people who can benefit by them. They are not intended to impress or attract everyone.

It is difficult for the casual observer to know who may deserve these signs. The spectator sees only the outward man or woman and does not know the effort they have given in this life or even past lives. Only the Lord knows their devotion. A miracle may indicate to the recipient the closeness of that person's bond to Sai Baba. It may be a sign to others of the faith and sincerity of the recipient. But if a seeker does not receive such signs, the seeker may still receive Sai's grace and protection.

I shall tell you why I give these rings, talismans, rosaries, etc. It is to signalize the bond between me and those to whom they are given. When calamity befalls them, the article comes to me in a flash and returns in a flash, taking from me the remedial grace of protection. That grace is available to all who call on me in any name or form, not merely to those who wear these gifts. Love is the bond that wins grace.

Sathya Sai Speaks 9, p. 84

There may be good reasons why a miracle would not be appropriate. For example, in the case of a miracle which heals an illness, the lessons of the illness must first be learned or the difficulty will only repeat itself. The divine sign must be suited specifically to the recipient. These Sai leelas (divine signs) are not idle acts intended to amaze the crowds. They hold great spiritual significance to the one they are intended for, often showing that person just how near and caring God is.

Sai Baba's miracles help us to recognize him. A startling experience is often required to shake us from our sleep. After we have learned of Baba's immeasurable love and wisdom, the miracles appear trivial. But to catch the attention of one caught in the grasp of the material world, they are indispensable. Only when we recognize the Lord will we heed his message.

I am determined to correct you only after informing you of my credentials. That is why I am now and then announcing my nature by means of miracles, that is, acts which are beyond human capacity and human understanding. Not that I am anxious to show off my powers. The object is to draw you closer to me, to cement your hearts to me.

Sathya Sai Speaks 2, p. 118

The world is God's leela, or play. No one can limit and define what is possible for the Lord. God's powers are beyond our comprehension. The miracles of Sai are now appearing around the globe. In virtually every country his presence is becoming known. A spiritual revolution of unparalleled proportions is taking hold. Yet Swami restrains publicity so that spiritual aspirants may still travel to see and experience him. In this age of rapid communication, it is a wonder that the name of Sai is not known by all.

> *Leelas are occurring throughout India in tens of millions of homes. Swami keeps his hand down so that publicity about the leelas will not spread. The rulers of the country know, but they keep it quiet. If the facts were to have publicity, millions would converge on Swami. The government would surround him with security guards, and devotees could not get close to him. The time is not ready.*
>
> *Conversations, p. 27*

Sai Baba's powers are tools for restoring truth, order, and love in the world. Sai Baba holds the power to manifest objects or make his presence known at great distances. He frequently creates sacred ash (vibhuti) or rings or lockets for his devotees. On several occasions, Swami has cured sickness or "taken over" the illness of a devotee. Sai Baba has even restored life to the dead. Indeed, his powers are beyond the limits of time and space. They are natural to him; they are not intended to attract or impress the curious.

> *You may infer from what you call my miracles that I am causing them to attract and attach you to me and me alone. They are not intended to demonstrate or publicize; they are merely spontaneous and concomitant proofs of divine majesty.*
>
> *Sathya Sai Speaks 6, p. 335*

Although Swami's powers seem capable of accomplishing anything, he does not make "quick fixes" for problems. People ask, "If Swami can change anything, then why does he not end hunger and sickness and all the evils of the world?" Swami says that if he were to change such things, they would only again revert to the way they were. He states that the minds and hearts of people need to be changed; only when individuals grow more loving and caring will the world change. Swami's way is slow but lasting. He limits his actions to conform to proper self-imposed restrictions.

> *Since Swami has taken a body, he has imposed certain proper limitations on himself. Swami has created idols of gold, and could just as easily create a mountain of gold. But then the Government would surround him and let nobody through.*
>
> *Conversations, p. 82*

4. Natural Power

Light and heat are natural aspects of the sun's power. Wetness and motion are inseparable from the ocean. Every being and object has attributes natural to its form and function. The divine power of creation is inherent in the Lord. The universe is the expression of his inventive will. When the Lord appears on earth, should he not naturally manifest this omnipotence?

Sathya Sai Baba did not acquire powers by means of spiritual disciplines (siddhi powers). Powers acquired by yogic means are not lasting, but Swami's powers have been with him all the years of his life. People new to Sai Baba sometimes denounce the miracles as improper, explaining that Ramakrishna warned against the use of such powers. Spiritual powers can be a hindrance to the aspirant, causing ego aggrandizement and other spiritual obstacles. This is a wise and true warning to all aspirants, but the difference is that Swami is not an aspirant. His powers are the natural facets of his divine being.

> *Some objects Swami creates in just the same way that he created the material universe. Other objects, such as watches, are brought from existing supplies. There are no invisible beings helping Swami to bring things. His sankalpa, his divine will, brings the object in a moment. Swami is everywhere. His creations belong to the natural unlimited power of God and are in no sense the product of yogic powers as with yogis or of magic as with magicians. The power is in no way contrived or developed, but is natural only.*
>
> *Conversations, pp. 104-105*

Swami advises devotees against practices to acquire any type of psychic powers. Powers would only add to our egoism and hinder our search for spiritual peace. Baba teaches that peace is found through love and service, not through such dangerous practices.

Once a yogi challenged Swami to an exhibition of powers. He knew that using Sai's name would increase his ticket sales and generate publicity. Of course, Baba paid no attention to this challenge. On the day of the exhibition, the yogi, who had claimed he could walk on water, stepped into a tank of water -- and sank. Of the incident, Swami said:

> *The man was walking on water. But ego and greed arose, and that finished it. Thought, word, and deed must be the same.*
>
> *Conversations, p. 71*

In contrast, Sai Baba's miracles are used only to teach spiritual lessons. He has never used his powers for his own benefit. Even as a small child, he made candy and pencils for other children, but never for himself. He lived in poverty, even using thorns to hold his shirt together when the buttons broke.

5. The Real Miracle

It is clear, as we come to understand the teachings of Sathya Sai Baba, that his real miracle is the transformation of our hearts. He transforms character and directs our lives along the spiritual path. There is little use for the manifestation of objects and signs except to awaken us and transform our personalities. Love is the real sign and miracle of Sai.

> *This prema (love) is my distinctive mark, not the creation of material objects or of health and happiness by sheer exercise of will. You might consider what you call miracles as the most direct sign of divinity, but the prema that welcomes you all, that blesses all, that makes me rush to the presence of the seekers, the suffering, and the distressed in distant lands or wherever they are, that is the real sign!*
>
> *Sathya Sai Speaks 6, p. 86*

Miraculous occurrences are only recognized by those who are ready to see the direction in which they point. To one for whom they are not intended, or to one not ready, they are disbelieved or simply ignored, for to see the truth behind such small signs is to see the spiritual truth itself and to find truth in oneself. Each new day is God's miracle, but to those unready it is just another day.

Questions for Study Circle

1. What is a miracle?
2. Are miracles necessary?
3. Why do miracles happen to some, but not to others?
4. Is it proper for Swami to perform miracles?
5. When and why should a miracle occur?
6. Why do miracles affect some people and not others?
7. What is the greatest miracle?
8. If you were able to perform physical miracles, would you?
9. Why does Sai Baba perform miracles?
10. What is the source of Baba's power?

References for Further Study

1. Conversations, p. 112 (Illnesses taken on for devotees).
2. My Baba and I, pp. 95-96 (Why instant solutions are not performed).
3. Sathya Sai Speaks 1, p. 113 (Miracles as calling cards).
4. Sathya Sai Speaks 4, p. 193 (Ramakrishna's reference to siddhi powers).
5. Sathya Sai Speaks 6, pp. 209-210 (Love is the greatest miracle).
6. Sathya Sai Speaks 7, p. 387 (Sai miracles come from divine power).
7. Sathya Sai Speaks 7, p. 388 (God can do anything).
8. Sathya Sai Speaks 8, p. 56 (Love is the greatest power).
9. Sathya Sai Speaks 9, p. 184 (Baba does not give powers to others).
10. Sathya Sai Speaks 9, p. 228 (Types of miracles).

11. Sathya Sai Speaks 10, p. 157 (The purpose of miracles).

12. Summer Showers 1974, p. 272 (Symbolism of vibhuti ash).

13. Summer Showers 1974, p. 282 (Miracles are an insignificant power of Sai).

14. Summer Showers 1974, pp. 286-288 (The purpose of rings and talismans).

CHAPTER TWENTY-TWO

Nonviolence: Recognition of Kinship

1. What Is Nonviolence?

Nonviolence is an attitude and practice of living in harmony with others and with oneself. It is living truthfully and doing one's duty with love and consideration. It is not a meek attitude of submission to the will of others; it can require the greatest bravery. Nonviolence requires adherence to high standards of truth and self-control.

Complete nonviolence is difficult to practice because all life has some elements of violence: we must eat even if we only eat plant matter; we must walk even though we may crush small insects. However, nonviolence is really an attitude in which we avoid inflicting pain on others. Even if we are unable to help others, we must at least refrain from intentionally harming them. Imagine the results if this simple rule were universally practiced.

2. Violence Is Ignorance of Unity

When we see a thorny plant in our path, we move to avoid it. Our eyes do not ignore the threat to the feet, for if the foot is pricked by thorns, the eyes will cry on their behalf. Just as the various organs of the body cooperate, all people and nations must cooperate. All creatures and all things together form the body of God. All share a common divine origin and destiny.

Spiritual understanding enables us to recognize the unity of all people as children of the Lord. All share the spark of God within. As the world becomes smaller through travel and communication, we can all realize how interconnected and interdependent people are. A disaster in one country may affect people in many lands. When we realize the truth of oneness, we feel the pain of others as our own.

> *Ahimsa (nonviolence) is another phase of sathya (truth). When once you are aware of the kinship, the oneness in God, the fundamental Atmic unity, no one will knowingly cause pain or distress to another.*
>
> *Sathya Sai Speaks 6, p. 128*

Doing violence to others is ultimately doing violence to oneself. We reap the consequences of our actions, whether in the present or future. The result is not always clearly seen, but the action evokes an inevitable reaction. When we injure another person, we often seek to justify our actions. Tacitus, a Roman historian, said, "It is a principle of human nature to hate those whom you have injured."

The best policy is to avoid harming others if at all possible. The safest rule is: "Do unto others as you would have them do unto you." Even small gestures can hurt another, hence we must be vigilant to avoid injuring others.

> It (nonviolence) does not mean merely not injuring a living being. You should not cause hurt even by a word, a look, or a gesture. Tolerance, fortitude, equanimity -- these help you to be steady in ahimsa.
>
> *Sathya Sai Speaks 10, p. 307*

Nonviolence must also extend to ourselves. Many people do greater violence to themselves than others could possibly do to them. They harm themselves through bad habits and improper living. They overemphasize negative events and get caught in the apparent evils of the world. They focus on darkness in the world, not allowing the light to enter.

Nonviolence must be a part of our perceptions and outlook. If we are unable to live peacefully with ourselves, it is impossible for us to live peacefully with others. The first step must be inner harmony and self-understanding. This develops as we strive to see divinity in all.

> We generally think that ahimsa (nonviolence) means not causing harm to some living being. Ahimsa is not just this. Even bad vision or bad hearing or bad talk is himsa (violence).
>
> *Summer Showers 1978, p. 210*

3. The Role of Duty

While adhering to our duty, we may possibly have to harm another. In the performance of his duty, a policeman may be required to harm a criminal who is violating the rights of others. A soldier may be required to harm others while defending his country. They do not seek to harm others, but their responsibility may require it. Their intention and duty must be considered.

If a dacoit (thief) cuts off your hand, it is himsa (violence); if the doctor amputates it, he saves your life and so it is ahimsa (nonviolence).

Sathya Sai Speaks 3, p. 117

The teachings of the Bhagavad Gita unfold in a drama that takes place on a battleground. In this battle, it is the duty of Arjuna to vanquish an unjust and violent foe. The Lord, Krishna, explains to Arjuna that it is his righteous duty to slay the enemy. Although the story has elements of an allegory, it is also an historical account of actual events.[1] Krishna, who always encouraged peaceful solutions, advised the warrior Arjuna to vanquish the evil Kauravas. The greater good of society required the elimination of the wicked foe.

Krishna wanted the peace of this world, and yet he encouraged this big battle in which forty lakhs of people were killed. Is this called himsa (violence) or ahimsa (nonviolence)? Even then, Krishna gave an appropriate answer to this. He said: "Arjuna! Let us take the case of a cancerous growth on the body, and this cancerous growth gives pain to the whole human body, although the growth itself is confined to a localized area...In this battle, or the operation, forty lakhs of disease-causing germs will be killed for the benefit of the world. Is this bad or is this for the good of the world?"

Summer Roses on the Blue Mountains, p. 23

On a smaller scale, we are sometimes compelled to harm small insects. In maintaining the order of the home, it may be necessary to eliminate ants, roaches, or various other small intruders. Swami explains that within the confines of the home, this is permissible.

H: Swami, one more question please, about household pests. The housewife is in a constant battle with ants, mosquitos, cockroaches, etc. Unless she fights, these insects take over her home.

SAI: It is all right, they must be dealt with.

---

1. *Conversations, pg. 118*

H: People are afraid they are committing a sin against Swami if they kill these small creatures.

SAI: There is nothing wrong in keeping the home free from the assault of these small creatures. But only where you are, your area. Not outside.

Conversations, p. 148

Sometimes we can avoid harming another creature by encouraging it to depart. Although we try to avoid striking another, we may have to "hiss" a little. An old Indian parable told by Ramakrishna illustrates this point.

There was once a small village that was terrorized by a large cobra. The serpent lurked in a dark area by the road and would strike out at any person who ventured too close. Finally, the situation became unbearable, so the villagers entreated a passing holy man to speak to the snake. The holy sadhu found the cobra in a terrible mood, but soon subdued him with mantras and kind words. He then spoke to the cobra and taught him the importance of nonviolence to his spiritual life.

This discourse completely changed the once-terrible serpent. He became quite docile and ate only fruit and milk. Soon the village children found that the snake would not attack them. The children became so bold as to swing the poor creature around by its tail. The serpent was soon reduced to a pitiable state, hiding by day and only venturing out at night for short periods. He lost weight and became bruised and battered.

When the holy man next ventured through that village to discover the progress of his snake disciple, he was told that the cobra was seldom seen -- and if so, then in a sad state of health. The holy man found the cobra cowering in a dark hole near his old haunt. Upon inquiring, he heard the sad story of the once-fearsome creature. He saw the abuse received by his serpent friend and chided him for his limited intelligence: "I said not to strike anyone. I did not say that you could not hiss!"

However, there may be times when even "hissing" is not enough. It may be necessary for us to harm another person if that person attacks us or those under our protection. Human life is very precious to each of us. We must take action to defend ourselves under extraordinary circumstances. If an attacker tries to kill us, we may have to injure or kill the assailant if all else fails. Of course, this would only be a last and highly regrettable action.

> *To preserve one's body is an important duty. One may take whatever means are necessary for self-preservation. About the other part of your question, to kill the person attacking -- the answer is yes, if that is the only way to preserve one's own life. But keep in mind that many alternative actions might be taken to avoid being killed. Only if every possibility is exhausted may one take the extreme measure of killing the attacker.*
>
> *My Baba and I, p. 187*

4. Intention and Attitude

Nonviolence is a matter of intention and attitude, directed from the heart. The heart must judge the individual situation and act with love and regard to duty. There must be compassion as well as a discriminating appraisal of the situation. If a creature is suffering without hope of succor, it may be proper to end its pain if no other solution can be found.

> *The meaning of ahimsa is that either in thought, word, or deed, you should not cause harm to anybody. Gandhi took a vow that till the end of his life, he would follow this. But on one occasion, when he saw a cow suffering from pain, he could not bear it and he advised the doctor to give an injection and end the life of the cow. Thus, in order to help the suffering individual, we may sometimes have to harm him.*
>
> *Summer Showers 1977, p. 235*

We are admonished to avoid doing violence to any creature whenever possible, and to respect all creatures as creations of the Lord. The inner voice is our best guide; it shows us our duty and obligations. So we must avoid harming others and act with compassion, in accordance with our responsibilities.

Questions for Study Circle

1. What is nonviolence?

2. Is the Bhagavad Gita fact or allegory?

3. Is there ever a time when killing is justified?

4. How do we practice nonviolence in daily living?

5. How can we deal with the violence of others?

6. Is nonviolence an attitude or action or both?

7. Why should we practice nonviolence?

8. Is it possible to be completely nonviolent?

9. How can we be nonviolent with ourself?

References for Further Study

1. Conversations, p. 20 (Eating meat).

2. Gita Vahini, p. 25 (Arjuna's duty to vanquish the Kauravas).

3. Gita Vahini, pp. 218-219 (Ahimsa, one of the twenty virtues for jnana).

4. Summer Showers 1978, p. 210.

5. Summer Roses on the Blue Mountains, pp. 23-24.

CHAPTER TWENTY-THREE

Suffering: Pain with a Purpose

1. Our Cue to Move On

Pain is a sign that something is wrong. When we feel bodily pain, we know that we have been injured or we are sick. It is a warning to us to examine the cause and repair the damage. Mental or emotional suffering is also an indication of need. It prompts us to change our attitudes and ideas. Joy is our natural state. No one is surprised when a baby is happy, but when the baby cries we rush to find and eliminate the cause.

Suffering is a reminder to us to press on until we reach the goal of self-realization. When we fall short of our spiritual aims, suffering reminds us that we have not yet dicovered our true nature of joy and wisdom. Suffering is a spur which starts us on the spiritual path and keeps us active in spiritual practice. It teaches us the lessons of loving wisdom and compassionate understanding. It impresses on us the need for strength and fortitude. Suffering is pain with a purpose; it alerts us to seek God-realization before our time expires.

> *It is grace; those who suffer have my grace. Only through suffering will they be persuaded to turn inward and make the inquiry. And without turning inward and making inquiry, they can never escape misery.*
>
> *Conversations, p. 110*

2. The Causes of Suffering

In India, a simple method is used to catch monkeys. A banana is placed inside a large pot that has a narrow neck. A curious monkey will come to examine the pot. When he discovers the fruit inside, he reaches in to grasp it. Holding the banana, he can no longer remove his hand through the narrow neck of the pot. In his greed, the unfortunate monkey will not let go of the fruit, even though it results in his capture.

We are like that monkey when we are held captive by our wrong desires. We grasp for material treasure, but in the long run our craving gives us only suffering. Selfish desire prevents us from being satisfied with ourselves as we are. It keeps us from realizing our true divine nature. We hold tantalizing images before our eyes and then we suffer because we cannot attain them. Desire keeps our minds spinning. It allows us no opportunity to find peace.

> *People suffer because they have all kinds of unreasonable desires and they pine to fulfill them and they fail. They attach too much value to the objective world. It is only when attachment increases that you suffer pain and grief.*
>
> *Sathya Sai Speaks 1, pp. 42-43*

Suffering also results from our past misdeeds. Through many lives lived in ignorance of spiritual principles, we have built a store of karma. The consequences of those previous actions pursue us like an unpaid debt. Through carelessness or evil intent, we may have added to the suffering of others, and even in this life the results seek us out. After the last log is thrown on a fire, the fire continues to burn for some time. But when we gain detachment, we can be unaffected by the heat. Usually suffering does not originate in external events; it stems from our attachment to results. Two people who suffer a similar loss may be affected very differently.

> *Strike a green tamarind fruit with a stone and you cause harm to the pulp inside, but strike the ripe fruit and see what happens. It is the dry rind that falls off; nothing affects the pulp or the seed. The ripe sadhaka (aspirant) does not feel the blows of fate or fortune; it is the unripe man who is wounded by every blow.*
>
> *Sathya Sai Speaks 4, p. 273*

Joy and suffering are inseparable companions. Both are natural consequences of our attachment to objects of desire. When we get the things we want, we are happy. If we do not get them, we are sad. When we acquire inner peace, we are not buffeted by the ups and downs of the world. We then acquire spiritual peace that is not conditioned by desire for earthly prosperity. With time, we learn to accept joy and grief with equal-mindedness. Then we avoid unnecessary suffering.

> *Joy and grief are the obverse and reverse of the same experience. Joy is when grief ends; grief is when joy ends. When you invite a blind man for dinner, you must set on the table two plates, for he comes along with another man who will lead him in. Grief and joy are inseparable companions.*
>
> *Sathya Sai Speaks 4, p. 85*

3. Tests of Character

We admire gnarled old trees that grow on lofty peaks or wave-pounded shores. Their twisted limbs and weathered bark paint a picture of courage and aspiration. Their roots dig into barren earth, clawing out an existence from near-barren beginnings. We respect such stalwarts far more than the pampered saplings of fertile valleys.

And yet we seek ease for ourselves. We resent the buffetings and salt spray that etch our own experience. We reject the hardships that endow us with our own unique character. But we must stand up to such trials. Our reaction to difficult situations is a test of our readiness to tread the spiritual path. How we deal with joy and suffering shows what we have learned and the strength we have developed.

Tests are a natural and necessary part of the razor-edged journey. Without tests, we would be unable to demonstrate our merit. Only by taking the tests can we pass on to higher stages. God, in his wisdom, does not let us graduate from one level without testing our fitness to move on. Progression to higher lessons too early would only result in the possibility of a fall later.

> *Being students, you know very well that the university has prescribed certain examinations at the end of every academic year. Do you ascribe this system to any desire for persecuting you? Do you think it is a sign of displeasure? You know that they are conducted so that you can be promoted, don't you? The yogis, sadhaks, and aspirants are being tested by God only to promote them.*
>
> *Sathya Sai Speaks 9, p. 72*

When we suffer difficult situations, we may feel that God does not see our plight. In fact, that is when God is watching us most closely. He gives us an opportunity to show our strength and fortitude. He watches closely to determine our faith in the face of obstacles. If we are to be given higher work, our strength must first be tested so that a disaster does not occur later.

> *Some of you feel neglected by me when disappointment or trouble comes upon you. But such obstacles alone can toughen your character and make your faith firm. When you hang a picture on the wall, you shake the nail and find out whether it is firm enough to bear the weight of the picture. So, too, in order to prevent the picture of God (his image in*

your mind and heart) from falling and being shattered to bits,
the nail (i.e., God's name) driven into the wall of the heart
has to be shaken to ascertain whether it is firm and steady.
                                          Sathya Sai Speaks 7, p. 444

4. An Opportunity for Growth

Birth is a painful experience for mother and child. Growth almost always involves some suffering. As we grow older, we learn many difficult lessons. Uncertainty and mistakes inevitably accompany new experience. However, that is no reason to avoid new experience. The pain of growth yields the satisfaction of progress. The comfort of stagnation gives way to the odor of decline.

By suffering the consequences of incorrect action, we eventually understand what gives lasting joy and what causes pain. We learn to appraise our actions and motivations more realistically. Material values recede and transpersonal values gain in importance. We see that through suffering we learn compassion and develop a sweet-tempered disposition. The needs of others grow in importance as our own become less important. The experience of pain and loss adds to our sweetness.

The sugarcane should welcome the cutting, the hacking and
the crushing, the boiling and the straining to which it is
subjected; without these ordeals, the cane would dry up and
make no tongue sweet. So, too, man must welcome trouble,
for that alone brings sweetness to the spirit within.
                                          Sai Baba Avatar, p. 58

When we suffer pain, it is usually for our benefit. If we are given a chance to pay for our misdeeds -- and take it -- we are truly attending to our spiritual growth. Grace prescibes the cure; pain is the taste of the medicine.

If a mother has two sons and one of them is sick, she will
give the sick son only bitter medicine, while she may give
the other son anything that he may ask for. If she gives bitter
medicine to one son and sweets to the other, it is not
because the mother likes one son more than the other. The
mother realizes that it is for the good of the sick child to take
bitter medicine, and so she gives him a bitter medicine, but
not because she likes him less.
                                          Sathya Sai Speaks 2, p. 153

5. Nearness to God

Perhaps the new devotee is surprised to find that all suffering does not end when one finds the Lord. When the initial discovery is made, we might believe that the future can hold only joy and peace. But this is an unreasonable expectation, soon dispelled. In fact, it is by the grace of the Lord that he points out our faults so that we may correct them.

It may be that our pain is increased as we progress more quickly through our "lessons." This is especially the case for "close devotees," who are seen as examples of Sathya Sai Baba's teachings. Each of us must live up to a high standard of behavior. An ideal devotee, such as Prahlada, may suffer as a lesson for others in faith and devotion. That devotee demonstrates the value of the spiritual path in developing equanimity. If we fail to exemplify the high ideals which we espouse, our punishment is strict, for the Lord has taken special interest in our progress and will not be satisfied with meager progress.

> *People, those outwardly "distant" from Swami, he tells, but not so severely as those "near." People judge Swami by his "near" devotees and so those individuals must follow very strict standards of behavior.*
>
> *Conversations, p. 111*

The Lord does not give his devotees more suffering than they can manage. The Lord protects and nurtures devotees on the path. Whatever suffering may come, it will not be more than the devotee can bear. The Lord is committed to the progress of his dear ones.

> *God protects his devotees. His devotee is near and dear to God, and he carries the devotee safely through life.*
>
> *Conversations, p. 48*

Inner peace alone confers lasting joy. The evanescent pleasures of the material world grant no lasting satisfaction. Our effort must be to experience the fountainhead of self-confidence and detachment which inspires us to greater spirituality. Our enthusiasm of today must grow into steady practice. Regular effort in the face of all obstacles ensures victory. Difficulties on the road must be welcomed as means to secure God's love and to demonstrate our worthiness to achieve higher goals.

> *You should not allow yourselves to be overwhelmed in any way by difficulties and sorrows, doubts and disappointments. You must have faith. Have confidence in*

yourself and strive to understand well the nature of God's love. To secure that love is the sacred goal of human life.
Sanathana Sarathi, Jan. 1985, p. 3

An easy and painless life would offer us little satisfaction. We would never know the exhilarating struggle for achievement or the sparkling joys of discovery. Although suffering is not a virtue and we should not seek it out, it does help us to understand the primacy of the spirit and the illusion of material glitter. Perhaps we should not be so quick to shun adversity, for through suffering alone do we realize the pain of attachment and the bliss of self-understanding.

Do you think I would confront you with pain were there not a reason for it? Open your heart to pain, as you do now to pleasure, for it is my will, wrought by me for your good. Welcome it as a challenge. Do not turn away from it. Do not listen to your mind, for mind is but another word for "need." The mind engenders need; it manifested as this world, because it needed this. It is all my plan, to drive you by the pangs of unfulfilled need to listen to my voice which, when heard, dissolves the ego and the mind with it.
Sanathana Sarathi, Aug.74, p. 185

Questions for Study Circle

1. Why do we suffer?

2. Does the Lord test us or do we test ourselves?

3. How can we avoid suffering when faced with tests and burdens?

4. Is it desirable to avoid suffering?

5. When we become a devotee of God, does suffering end?

6. Is it possible to learn life's lessons without suffering?

7. Is it possible to have joy without grief?

8. Can we know the cause of our suffering?

9. Is suffering a result of inner attitude or outer events?

10. Is attachment related to suffering?

References for Further Study

1. Conversations, p. 103 (The suffering of saints as an example for us).

2. Conversations, pp. 110-111.

3. Sathya Sai Speaks 2, p. 153 (Rise up to demands of the test and please the Lord).

4. Sathya Sai Speaks 3, p. 20 (Baba takes over the stroke of a devotee).

5. Sathya Sai Speaks 5, p. 230 (Tests give confidence).

6. Sathya Sai Speaks 6, p. 261 (Hardships teach us).

7. Sathya Sai Speaks 9, pp. 71-76 (Tests).

8. Summer Showers 1974, pp. 102-104 (God introduces an occasional test to determine our strength).

9. Summer Showers 1974, pp. 288-289.

10. Summer Showers 1977, p. 2 (Joy and sorrow are inseparable).

11. Summer Showers 1977, p. 140 (People pay more attention to the pain than to the joy of life).

12. Summer Showers 1978, p. 32.

13. Summer Showers 1978, p. 166 (Prahlada's suffering).

CHAPTER TWENTY-FOUR

Surrender: Fullness of Faith

1. To Whom Do We Surrender?

The word surrender does not properly describe the Sanskrit word saranagathi. The Sanskrit word connotes surrender in terms of devotion to God and acceptance of his divine will. It implies not a surrender to some other person, but surrender to our own inner divinity.

On the spiritual path, no one should be asked to relinquish their judgment or to accept ideas blindly. Nothing could be further from the truth. We must test all spiritual teachings with our own experience. To reach the goal of liberation, we must evaluate the benefits of all doctrines for ourselves. Surrender does not require discarding the intellect; it requires heightened spiritual discrimination. Surrender to God is surrender to our God-oriented aspirations -- to our own God-nature, the atma.

> *It is not a question of surrendering or giving to some other one. One surrenders to oneself. Recognition that the atma is oneself is surrender. Surrender really means the realization that all is God, that there is nobody who surrenders, that there is nothing to be surrendered, nor is there anyone to accept a surrender. All is God. There is only God.*
>
> *Conversations, p. 93*

2. What Is Surrendered?

What do we have that we can surrender to God? Everything is his already. The flower which we offer at his feet is plucked from his garden. The service which we offer is his gift to us. Our "surrender" is actually our acceptance of divine will. It is renunciation of the illusion of separateness. It is abandonment of the ego that says, "This is mine."

Surrender requires us to discard all that does not bring us closer to God-realization. Our attachments and desires for material acquisitions and emotional satisfactions must be released. We must perform action without desire for the results; the results rest in God's hands.

*Surrendering to the Lord is surrendering all thoughts and
actions, not wishing for the fruits of the action, not doing
action to gain its fruit, but doing the action because it is one's
duty. The act is dedicated to the Lord and the results,
therefore, are borne by the Lord.*

Conversations, pp. 13-14

3. Why Surrender?

Why not surrender? All that we possess to renounce are the desires
which bind us to the wheel of rebirth. The only attachments we hold are
the reins of wild horses, which pitch us through the muck and brambles
of desire. What have we gained from our headlong plunge into
worldliness? Has it resulted in greater peace? What have we acquired
that will not be taken away by Yama, the god of death?

And yet surrender is so difficult. It defies the cravings of the ego.
Like the strong man in the circus, the ego enthralls us with his carnival
antics. The mind is characterized by desire, chief assistant to the ego.
This desire keeps us distant from our true, loving, and joyful self. It is
natural for the mind to seek happiness outside of itself. It seeks
happiness in objects, in places, in other people -- in anything but inner
self-sufficiency. Like the fool seeking everywhere for the glasses that
rest upon his own nose, truth, bliss, and its derivatives such as joy and
happiness can only be found in the atma.

*The discontented man is as bad as lost. Rely on the Lord
and accept whatever is your lot. He is in you, with you. He
knows best what to give and when. He is full of prema (love).*

Sathya Sai Speaks 6, p. 176

Life is happier when we leave results to God. Only the Lord knows
what we deserve. He knows the past, present, and future of each. He
knows our strengths and weaknesses and how to deliver us to our
specific goal. The pilgrimage is quicker and easier if the path is left to
him.

Resign yourself into God's hands. Let him give success or failure, what does it matter? He may be bent upon toughening you, or it may be for your good in the long run. How can you judge? Who are you to judge? Why judge?

Sathya Sai Speaks 3, p. 93

Happiness is found when we discard wrong desires and attachment. When we live in the present, in the eternal now, we discard our fears and hopes, allowing divinity to shine through. Joy needs no object; it is our own nature. We must leave the transformation to the Lord. Our only duty is to play our part well; the results are not our burden.

When you travel by train, you have only to purchase the ticket, enter the proper train, and take a seat, leaving the rest to the engine. Why should you carry the bed and trunk on your head? So, too, put your trust in the Lord and carry on to the best of your ability.

Sathya Sai Speaks 1, p. 166

4. Surrender Must Be Complete

We are undergoing an operation for the removal of inflamed ego. The illusory organ must be removed because it threatens to end spiritual life. After consultation and some second opinions, we have chosen the surgeon -- Sathya Sai Baba. Now we must submit to his program. It will not be possible for us to review each incision and suture. We have neither the knowledge nor the skill to judge his method. We must be content to view the recovery room full of happy survivors. If we insist on examining each step of the operation, we can only muddle the procedure.

Surrender to God's will is the safest path. However, surrender must be real and complete. When we depend on the Lord, the Lord takes care of our needs and delivers us to our goal. The Lord provides all that we require for the journey.

Surrender to me only. When that surrender is complete and all acts, words, and thoughts are dedicated to the Lord along with all their consequences, then he has promised that he will free you from sin and sorrow.

Sathya Sai Speaks 5, p. 54

If we maintain a big ego, our efforts are doomed to failure. We cannot take credit for the victories and ascribe our defeats to the will of God.

But if we truly leave the results to God, God takes responsibility for us and speeds us on our way.

> *It depends on the people involved. In the case of a devotee who has pure thoughts and a pure heart and who has surrendered to Bhagavan, then Swami takes full responsibility for that life and takes care of that devotee. But where a person has a big ego, relying on ego desire and not on Bhagavan, then Swami keeps a distance and does not interfere.*

Conversations, p. 131

Complete surrender earns God's love. When we devote all our time and energy to the Lord, he moves closer to us. When we take one step toward God, he takes ten steps toward us.

> *When you want the love of the Lord, you should be fully prepared to completely surrender yourself to the Lord. You should have no attachment to your body or pay attention to your honor or respect. You should completely detach yourselves from all these. Only then can you get close to the Lord.*

Summer Showers 1978, p. 94

5. The Guards at the Gate

When we practice surrender, we must exercise patience and fortitude. It is not possible for us to demonstrate surrender to God's will in one day. The Lord tests his devotees to measure the degree of their faith and strength. And so we must constantly remember to trust the Lord. It is not up to us to judge what is good or bad. Surrender must be real, not a practice followed only if it yields quick results. Surrender requires acceptance of suffering as well as joy, defeat as well as victory. With time we will reach our Atmic destiny, but effort and patience are needed on the way.

> *If you want to enter the palace of moksha, or liberation, you will find that at the main entrance there are two guards. This entrance is the place where you offer yourself, and it may be called the gate of surrender. The two guards who are*

there are called Srama (effort) and Dama
(patience)...However much you offer yourself in surrender,
it is not possible for you to enter God's abode without Srama
and Dama.

Summer Showers 1973, pp. 129-130

6. Expressway to Success

The practice of spiritual surrender is a complete sadhana (spiritual path). It is sufficient by itself to ensure self-realization. Complete surrender requires a range of spiritual disciplines for its success. Control of the ego is essential, and with that control come humility and equanimity. Surrender requires faith and devotion to the Lord. Faith engenders fearlessness and devotion nurtures love for all God's creatures. Patience and effort contribute to the accomplishment. These qualities ensure a life of service to others.

At the end of our journey, we find that the goal was always within our reach. There was no other one to surrender to, for our own nature is God. There is nothing to be known and nothing to be done. There is none other than God in all the wide creation.

So long as there is this distinction in the mind of the
individual between God on the one hand and 'I' of the
individual on the other hand, this cannot be accepted as
complete surrender. So long as this duality is evident, one
cannot accept the situation as complete surrender.

Summer Showers 1972, p. 104

The constant remembrance of God enables us to see God in all, for everything is the play of the Lord. When we remember the Lord always, we see him in all things. No more is required from us than sincere faith and patience. Surrender requires no special qualifications or prerequisites -- just trust in the Lord.

As a sign of this deed of surrender and in order to sustain
it, nothing more is enjoined than constant remembrance of
the name. No regimen of exhausting sadhana is prescribed.
Smarana (remembrance) is enough.

Sathya Sai Speaks 9, p. 41

Questions for Study Circle

1. What is surrender?
2. What are the benefits of surrender?
3. Is surrender indifference?
4. Does surrender imply lack of judgment?
5. Do we surrender to God or to ourselves?
6. Does surrender make us dependent on God?
7. Is surrender a sign of spiritual growth?
8. If we practice surrender, must we do any other spiritual practice?
9. Will God take care of all our needs if we surrender to him?
10. How do we know if we have truly surrendered?
11. What is surrendered?

References for Further Study

1. Conversations, pp. 13-14, 130-131.
2. Gita Vahini, pp. 170-175 (The pundit and the king).
3. Sathya Sai Speaks 5, p. 12 (Surrender the ego and God will ensure liberation).
4. Sathya Sai Speaks 5, pp. 52-53 (The stages of wisdom).
5. Sathya Sai Speaks 6, p. 89.
6. Sathya Sai Speaks 7, p. 376 (Surrender even your judgment to the Lord).
7. Sathya Sai Speaks 7, pp. 464-465 (If you are God, to whom do you surrender?).
8. Sathya Sai Speaks 9, p. 41 (The surrender of Lakshmana).
9. Summer Showers 1972, pp. 101-104 (What is surrender?).
10. Summer Showers 1972, p. 113 (Arjuna was taught the Bhagavad Gita because he had surrendered).

11. Summer Showers 1972, pp. 248-249 (God takes care of the responsibilities of one fully surrendered to him).

12. Summer Showers 1973, p. 206 (If one surrenders to God, one will be happy).

13. Summer Showers 1973, p. 246.

14. Summer Showers 1974, pp. 30-31.

15. Summer Showers 1977, p. 166 (Vibhishana's surrender).

CHAPTER TWENTY-FIVE

Peace: Oneness with God

1. Virtue Is Peace

Peace is like a well-channeled river. It does not rest in a static state; rather, it harmoniously adapts to change. Although a river constantly flows, it maintains an equilibrium with the shore. From obscure mountain origins, it plunges to the plains, assuming a name, and then it merges namelessly in the vast ocean. Peace also flows and grows; it is the sign of God's creation working in harmony.

Peace for spiritual aspirants is a state of equanimity based on understanding of and adherence to dharma (spiritual duty). When we understand the divine basis for creation and live in accordance with it, we can move unruffled by the currents of daily events. Recognition of divinity in all creatures and all objects grants us courage and confidence. When we lead virtuous lives, leaving the results of our actions to God, we experience peace.

> *When man thinks, speaks, and acts along virtuous lines, his conscience will be clean and he will have inner peace. Knowledge is power, it is said; but virtue is peace.*
>
> *Sathya Sai Speaks 10, p. 267*

To experience peace, we must master our unreasonable expectations. Agitation usually results from unfulfilled desires, not from external conditions. The mind creates wrong desire when it loses control over the senses. Virtue requires us to hold the senses in check. If we hold to material values, we lose our inner peace. If we live virtuously, we grow into unbounded joy.

> *What exactly is peace? It is the stage in which the senses are mastered and held in balance.*
>
> *Sanathana Sarathi, Jan. 1985, p. 11*

A controlled mind enables us to rest, content with the present, not dwelling on the past or expecting too much from the future. When the endless progression of thoughts is controlled, the divine purity of consciousness shines forth. The mind should be a tool of the atma, the inner divinity. The mind should not become our master, roaming unchecked among the objects of desire. The mind creates desire, so it must be taught to remain quiet when it is not required for a specific task. Like a small child, it must be taught to limit its reach and to rest occasionally.

> *There is some small confusion of terms, for there is no mind as such. The mind is a web of desires. Peace of mind is no desires, and in that state there is no mind. Mind is destroyed, so to speak. Peace of mind really means purity, complete purity of consciousness.*

Conversations, p. 44

2. Our Real Nature

A tiger cub was once separated from its mother and lost in the forest. It happened to come upon a gathering of goats and joined them for companionship. After some time, the cub began to eat grass and behave like the goats with which it lived. It bleated and pranced just like the others. This went on for months, until the herd was spied by the mother tigress. She pounced upon the group, scattering them in all directions. The young tiger cub bleated and dashed for cover in panic. However, the tigress noticed the incongruous "goat" and chased it down.

Dragging the terrified cub to a water hole, she instructed it to look into the water. The cub was amazed to find that he looked just like the fearsome tigress, not the goats with which he had associated. He was, after all, a master of the forest himself.

We tend to be grass-eating tigers. We have come to believe that we are something less than divinity. If we look into the pool of spiritual truth, we find that we are the very source of wisdom, love, and peace. When we still the mind, it will cease to delude us into believing that we are less than what we are -- the atma.

Atmic peace is our true nature; it is acquired when we look within. If we are concerned only with outer circumstances, the jumble of daily events, we will be unable to experience peace. Ignorance of our divine origin causes us to be elated or dejected at the changing course of events. Our true nature is selfless love and joyful peace, unbounded by time or circumstance. It manifests when it is allowed to shine through the clouds of illusion.

Once you enter the depths of the sea, it is all calm, it is all peace. Agitation, noise, confusion -- all are only on the outer layers. So also in the innermost recesses of the heart, there is a reservoir of santhi (peace) where you must take refuge.
Sathya Sai Speaks 1, p. 172

The possibility of acquiring inner peace is not so distant as we may think. In fact, all people possess it already. Peace is our essential nature, but it is hidden by the clouds of attachment. Peace is like the sun, always shining, but temporarily covered by the darkness of anger or selfishness. The divine self, the atma, radiates peace and joy. We need only to look within for the source of our joy.

Peace and joy can be secured only by realizing that they are one's own real nature.
Sathya Sai Speaks 6, p. 58

3. Inner Peace, Outer Peace

Faith results in a peaceful outlook. As rose-colored glasses turn everything that color, inner peace sets our own "world" at peace. When we discern the divine basis for creation, we cease to be upset by changing circumstances. Faith in God and faith in oneself set one's world at rest.

So real santhi (peace) is to be had only in the depths of the spirit, in the discipline of the mind, in faith in the one base of all this seeming multiplicity. When that is secured, it is like having gold: you can have any variety of ornaments made from it.
Sathya Sai Speaks 1, p. 124

When we wear comfortable shoes, even the bumpiest roads seem smooth. Although the track may be covered with small stones or glass, we can walk without fear. Wherever we travel, on highway or trail, we are assured of a smooth journey. Peace within protects us in the same way. Inner peace reflects outwardly as peace in our own immediate world. What we perceive in our surroundings is a reflection of our inner state. If we realize the joy and beauty within ourselves, we also perceive it in the realm around us. Peace is a cloak which affords us comfort even on the coldest days.

So, too, the man who is at peace with himself will discern peace all around him. Nature is beauty, truth, peace. Man sees it ugly, false, and violent -- that is all.
                                                    Sathya Sai Speaks 9, p. 147

Peace in the world depends on peace in each individual. No laws or treaties can bring about peace without righteousness in individuals. Righteousness results when individuals master their unreasonable desires. With proper understanding, they leave the results of action to God and act in accordance with their spiritual duty.

If there is righteousness in the heart

There will be beauty in the character.

If there is beauty in the character

There will be harmony in the home.

When there is harmony in the home,

There will be order in the nation.

When there is order in the nation,

There will be peace in the world.
                                                    Sathya Sai Speaks 7, pp. 189-190

Righteousness in the heart results from the vision of Oneness. People of all lands share the same divine status as embodiments of God. When all recognize that the same God-nature moves in each, they will respect one another. All are waves on the ocean of God, not separate from each other or from God.

Now all things have gone up in value; man alone has become cheap...He has become cheaper than animals; he is slaughtered in millions without any qualm because of the terrific growth in anger, hate, and greed; he has forgotten his unity with all men, all beings, and all worlds. The contemplation of that unity alone can establish world peace, social peace, and peace in the individual.
                                                    Sathya Sai Speaks 4, p. 287

4. How Do We Cultivate Peace?

To gain a true perspective on an object, we need to move away from it. If we are too close, we are confused by its motion or the details of its appearance. When we stand on the shore, the ocean may appear angry and restless, but from space it is a calm blue pond. Our closeness -- or our attachment -- to objects robs us of our peace. When objects are near, mentally, emotionally, or physically, we are more likely to relate to them on an ego level. We are apt to interpret them in terms of our own personality. To cultivate peace we must move back and detach from objects.

When we calm our emotions and center ourselves within, we gain control of our minds. Peace grants us perspective for intelligent action. In fact, peace encourages many virtues. It grants divine vision, which encourages wisdom and love.

> *Santhi (peace) is essential for sharpness of intellect. Santhi develops all the beneficial characteristics of man. Even farsightedness grows through santhi. Through that, obstacles and dangers can be anticipated and averted.*
>
> *Prasanthi Vahini, p. 12*

The vision of unity is won by intense spiritual practice. Practice helps us to see God in everything and in everyone. That vision results from clearly analyzing the results of thoughts and actions. When we see the painful consequences of desires for fleeting pleasures and material acquisitions, we learn to search for more lasting values. Then we experience the joy and peace derived from knowing God.

> *Only thoughts of God and intense love for him bring peace. As worldly thoughts diminish, thoughts of God increase. Normally, the mind desires these worldly things all the time. As the desires are cut one by one, the peace becomes stronger...When there are Godly thoughts, there is peace of mind. Swami cannot give peace of mind; one has to work for it.*
>
> *Conversations, p. 22*

Until the mind is stilled and peace is experienced, we must engage the mind in pure thoughts. We must have faith that God will give us our due. The Lord dispenses results in accordance with what we have earned. If we leave the results to God, we can experience peace. Centered on God, we are content with whatever may happen.

But you cannot easily detach yourself from activity; the mind clings to some thing or other. Make it cling to God, let it do all things for God and leave the success or failure of the thing done to God, the loss and profit, the elation and dejection. Then you have the secret of santhi and contentment.

Sathya Sai Speaks 4, p. 318

Questions for Study Circle

1. What is peace?

2. Is peace possible with any kind of external conditions?

3. Does peace come from within or from without?

4. How is peace cultivated in daily life?

5. Is peace a state of mind, emotion, or circumstance?

6. Does God grant peace?

7. How can peace in the world be achieved?

8. What are the obstacles to inner peace?

9. How do we act without attachment?

10. Does peace mean lack of effort?

11. Is peace natural to human beings?

12. Can we make spiritual progress if we have too much peace?

References for Further Study

1. Prasanthi Vahini, p. 10 (Peace is won by recalling the travails of the saints and sages).

2. Prasanthi Vahini, p. 11 (Peace is the nature of man. Anger and greed suppress it).

3. Sathya Sai Speaks 6, p. 231 (First learn inner peace, then you can deal with the world).

4. Sathya Sai Speaks 7, p. 407 (Action without attachment to the fruits brings peace).

5. Sathya Sai Speaks 8, p. 32 (Peace can only come from within).

6. Summer Showers 1977, p. 24 (True peace is in the heart).

CHAPTER TWENTY-SIX

Devotion: The Vision of Love

1. What Is Devotion?

Devotion is a mystery of the heart. No amount of argument could persuade us to feel devotion toward the Lord, for it is a bond between the creator and the created which surpasses rational understanding. Perhaps it is in our nature to feel and express devotion. It may result from lifetimes of spiritual striving. Actually, devotion is comprised of many feelings, emotions, and thoughts. It includes gratitude, reverence, adoration, love, thanksgiving, even fear of sin, but ultimately all descriptions must fail. For, in truth, devotion is only understood when it is experienced.

> *The Lord is understood only by the bhakta (devotee); the bhakta is understood only by the Lord.*
>
> *Sandeha Nivarini, p. 58*

2. The Path of Love

The spiritual path of devotion to God (bhakti yoga) is one of the three primary approaches to self-realization, which are outlined in Hindu thought. The other paths are the way of selfless action (karma yoga) and the way of wisdom (jnana yoga). On each path, the aspirant seeks to reduce ego and merge with the divine principle. If we aspire to God-realization, we enlarge our vision to include everything within ourselves. Bondage is ended when we realize there is nothing apart from ourselves; we are the universal absolute.

The bhakti devotee strives to realize God by reducing ego to nothing. When our ego disappears, only God is left. Devotion promotes humility and surrender to divine will. On the path of devotion, the Lord himself guides us to our goal.

> *The ego is most easily destroyed by bhakthi (devotion); by dwelling on the magnificence of the Lord and by humility and service to others as children of the Lord.*
>
> *Sathya Sai Speaks 1, p. 60*

In this era of spiritual decline, devotion is said to be the safest and easiest path for most people to realize God. The devotee's loving surrender to God draws God to the devotee. The devotee is like a thirsty kitten crying for its mother; the mother responds to the kitten's entreaty to relieve its need. Similarly, the Lord responds to those who depend on him and selflessly love him.

The seeker of wisdom, the jnani, aspires to freedom through the exercise of intuitive wisdom. To merge with formless Oneness, this seeker relies on experiential cognition of divinity. The jnani surrenders reason to the direct perception of God-consciousness. In this age, the path of wisdom is difficult for most seekers. It is easy for the jnani to become caught up in his own scholarship or asceticism. The path requires rare clarity of mind from a seeker, particularly in the absense of qualified teachers.

The way of action, karma yoga, is based upon the aspirant's selfless service to others. The karma yogi serves the Lord in the forms of other people and creatures. This seeker exercises patience and equanimity to break down the walls of egoism. By concentrating on the needs of others, the karma yogi removes the barriers to liberation. The potential difficulty of this path is the aspirant's pride in his or her accomplishments in the field of service.

The major benefit of the devotional path in this age is that it avoids the pitfalls of pride. Our era is characterized by personal pride and self-aggrandizement. For this reason, the bhakti path is considered safest. When we fully surrender to the Lord, the Lord delivers us to our goal; there is no need for us to worry.

> *Bhakti is the through-carriage. Though it may be detached from one train and connected to another, if you get into it, you need not worry; so long as you stick to your place, it is bound to take you to your destination.*
>
> *Sathya Sai Speaks 3, p. 134*

3. Requisites for Success

Success in devotion does not require adherence to any particular creed or religion. The devotee should act only with love toward all. That love reaches God, by whatever name one calls him. If we perform our spiritual duty, God's grace naturally flows to us. When devotion manifests in action and virtuous character, we may be sure that it is genuine. It is not enough if we preach virtue, but do not practice the messages of love and truth.

> *The devotion of an individual is open to suspicion if he has love for God but does not pay heed to God's word. Desire for God but neglect of his injunctions cannot be the true characteristic of devotion.*
>
> *Summer Showers 1979, p. 42*

Fervent devotion to the Lord is a good first step, but its effect is limited if it is not tempered with discipline and duty. Our love for the Lord is important, but it is more important for him to love us. We draw God's love to ourselves by performing our duties well and living within the bounds of right conduct.

> *Imbibe the ideals of duty, devotion, and discipline. Devotion must be tested in the crucible of discipline. It must be directed along the lines of duty.*
>
> *Sathya Sai Speaks 9, p. 220*

If we restrict our worship to the church or temple one day a week, we will realize only limited success. Devotion is a full-time pursuit. It requires commitment to achieving the goal of realization, of seeing divinity at all times and in all places. Self-transformation requires constant practice. It must be steady in the face of all obstacles.

> *When grief overtakes you, you run to God...When joy is restored you throw him overboard...Bhakti is not a temporary salve. It is the unbroken contemplation of God without any other interposing thought or feeling.*
>
> *Gita Vahini, p. 223*

4. How to Start

To arrive at the destination of universal love, we must embark on the path of individual love. No single relationship to the Lord is suitable for all devotees, but all can love God in their own way. One person may assume the attitude of a child toward its parent. Another may see God as a companion or close friend. Any positive type of relationship or attitude enables us to draw closer to God. All forms of devotion are accepted by the Lord when expressed with love.

There are different modes of devotion: that which foolishly weeps for me when I am not physically present; that which surrenders with wild abandon; and that which is steady and strong, ever attached to my will. I accept all these forms of devotion. The choice between one or the other is not yours, for it is I who rule your feelings, modifying them. If you try to go where I do not will, I will stop you; you can do nothing apart from my will. Be assured of that: this is the highest devotion.

Sanathana Sarathi, Aug. 1974, p. 185

Devotion begins with selfish love, but with time and practice, it develops into universal love. When we no longer seek return for love given, we can love all beings as expressions of God's omnipresence, for God resides in all beings. When we discover God within ourselves, we also find God in all creatures and all things. As our hearts open to God's love, we become love, and we see the world through the "glasses" of love. Devotion may bud with the adoration of a picture or image in a temple, but it blossoms in the vision of love without limit. That vision confers faith and strength, which speeds us to our goal.

There is only one royal road for the spiritual journey -- love, love for all beings as manifestations of the same divinity that is the very core of oneself. This faith alone can ensure the constant presence of God within you and endow you with all the joy and courage you need to fulfill the pilgrimage to God.

Sanathana Sarathi, June 83, p. 159

Devotion is cultivated by slow and steady effort. It must grow strong and certain to support character. A quick rush forward will not help us if we only fall back again when our resolve is tested. Progress must be protected by discrimination, which knows its own strength.

When the tender plant of devotion begins to grow, it must be protected. When a young tree is growing, various animals will eat it and may kill it. For this reason, a fence is placed around the young tree to protect it. When the tree is grown, it needs no protection. The same animals who would have first destroyed it, now seek and find shade and shelter beneath its branches. When devotion has grown strong and intense, it will burn all sins.

Conversations, p. 69

5. Perseverance -- The Guarantee of Accomplishment

Devotion requires our fortitude and tenacity. Through hardships, we build strength. We may feel devotion when life is happy, but maintaining devotion through difficult circumstances is the true test. Hurdles appear in dealing with family and friends. Overcoming our own inertia is also difficult. But true devotion is like tempered steel: it is strengthened and purified by the fire of adversity. When we acquire spiritual strength, we can encourage others.

> *Because of many obstacles and troubles that came to Prahlada and because of the punishments that were given him, it was possible for the rest of the world to know how great Prahlada's devotion was.*
>
> *Summer Roses on the Blue Mountains, p. 26*

We should welcome troubles as tests to prove our devotion. Tests provide an opportunity to remove karmic obstacles that hold us back. Even the finest gold must be melted and hammered to give it shape; so also the rough diamond only gains in value when it is cut and polished. True devotion remains constant and full in the face of adversity.

> *God is ignored in sunshine; he is wanted only when there is night. Devotion must persist and flourish, unaffected by time, place, or circumstance.*
>
> *Sathya Sai Speaks 9, p. 121*

6. God, One Without Second

The Lord guides and protects us when we surrender to his will. He bestows his grace to save us from harm. To win grace, however, we must immerse ourselves in God and strive to do his will.

> *It is God's word that if you have devotion to God, he will look after all your future. He will look after all the welfare that is due to you.*
>
> *Summer Showers 1972, p. 105*

To earn God's full-time protection requires full-time devotion. Many seekers spend little time in prayer, meditation, or service, but they expect God's grace to flow always in their direction. To earn that protection requires constancy of effort.

In an office, if you work full time, you get full pay. If you work part-time, you get half pay. Today, we show only part-time devotion and we want full-time reward for this part-time devotion. How can we get this?

Summer Showers 1973, p. 179

Devotion to God must be single-minded for it to be effective. The magnifying glass can ignite a fire because it concentrates the sun's rays at a single point. Concentrated devotion burns away all obstacles to liberation, even in this lifetime.

Concentration on God with a fragmented mind is an exercise in futility. Single-minded devotion is the easiest path to salvation. In fact, the ananyabhakta (one-pointed devotee) becomes a jivanmukta (one liberated during life.)

Summer Showers 1979, p. 151

The culmination of full-time devotion is seeing God in all things. Then all events and beings are seen in a divine light. Nothing is separate from God, for when we are filled with God, we see only God. Then we know beyond doubt that we have reached the summit of practice. We experience joy and peace beyond measure.

Bhakti is the state of mind in which one has no separate existence apart from God. His very breath is God; his every act is by God, for God; his thoughts are of God; his words are uttered by God, about God. For like the fish which can only live in water, man can only live in God -- in peace and happiness.

Sathya Sai Speaks 6, p. 119

Questions for Study Circle

1. What is devotion?

2. Who is a devotee of the Lord?

3. Is emotion part of devotion?

4. Does devotion make a person impractical?

5. If we are God, then to whom do we express devotion?

6. Is realization possible without devotion?

7. How is devotion cultivated?

8. How do we know if we have real devotion?

9. Is it possible to gauge another's devotion?

10. What are the benefits of devotion?

11. What is the goal of devotion?

References for Further Study

1. Gita Vahini, pp. 197-204.

2. Gita Vahini, p. 198 (It is more important for the Lord to love you than for you to love the Lord).

3. Prasanthi Vahini, p. 18 (The path of devotion is most conducive to success).

4. Prasanthi Vahini, p. 19 (Some saints' descriptions of bhakti).

5. Prema Vahini, p. 21 (How to cultivate devotion).

6. Prema Vahini, p. 22 (Image worship).

7. Sathya Sai Speaks 1, p. 50 (Stages of devotion).

8. Sathya Sai Speaks 2, p. 137 (A devotee is one rooted in faith).

9. Sathya Sai Speaks 3, p. 199 (The real basis for devotion).

10. Sathya Sai Speaks 4, p. 85 (The difficulty of devotion).

11. Sathya Sai Speaks 6, pp. 140-142 (The king who had a vision of Radha and Krishna).

12. Sathya Sai Speaks 10, p. 72 (The devotee and the jnani).

13. Sathya Sai Speaks 10, p. 175 (Types of devotion).

14. Sathya Sai Speaks 11, pp. 238-244, 246-249 (Types of devotion).

15. Summer Showers 1972, p. 258 (In the Kali Yuga, devotion is the only means to attain liberation).

16. Summer Showers 1974, p. 106 (God is as close to you as you are close to him).

17. Summer Showers 1977, p. 165 (Without devotion, you can achieve nothing).

18. Summer Showers 1978, pp. 149-150 (Madhura bhakti).

19. Summer Showers 1978, pp. 194-197 (Pushti, maryada and pravaha bhakti).

20. Summer Showers 1979, p. 151 (Single-minded devotion).

21. Summer Roses on the Blue Mountains, p. 99 (Education and service are of limited value without devotion).

22. Summer Roses on the Blue Mountains, pp. 106-114.

CHAPTER TWENTY-SEVEN

Service: A Gift of Love

1. A Meaningful Contribution

Charitable service is a component of all major religions. Even people who have no religious affiliation often feel the call to serve others. There is, in most of us, an innate recognition that we are part of society and that we are dependent on and obligated to society.

We also have a fundamental urge to find meaning in life. This urge translates into our desire to contribute to our community. We feel that we should leave the Earth a better place than when we arrived. It is our duty to repay our debt to society and to improve the situation of others. If we will not serve God in the forms of our unfortunate brothers and sisters, how can we seek to realize a formless God?

If you cannot pray for the total welfare of the community around you in whom God lives, how is it possible for you to worship an invisible God? The first thing you have to do is to look after the welfare of the living community around you.
Summer Showers 1974, p. 218

2. Service to Self

A sculptor carves off small chips to reveal a statue latent in a block of wood. His efforts gradually result in the emergence of a graceful figure that all can appreciate. It could be said that his skill was used for the benefit of the figure or for the joy of the viewer of the form. But it would be more accurate to say that it was for his own benefit. Each line and curve produced in the wood revealed the image he held within. The effort revealed his skill and the beauty of his vision. It resulted in his own satisfaction.

If we serve, thinking that our action is primarily for the benefit of others, we are incorrect. Service holds the greatest benefit for the one who serves. Others are assisted, but we derive the joy and spiritual lessons from the act. We come to recognize ourselves in others, which widens our compassion and broadens our vision.

Service expands our vision beyond our own small ego boundaries. How can we be joyful when those beside us suffer? How can we see their pain and not respond? As we grow spiritually, we recognize that brotherhood is a reality, not simply a pious-sounding theory of churchgoers.

> *If the individual is deluded into believing that he is saving others, then woe be to him, for there is no other at all. All are One; one man's sorrow is everyone's sorrow. The fundamental flaw is the ignorance of man. If only he was wise, he would have known that all individuals are waves on the surface of the selfsame ocean.*
>
> *Sathya Sai Speaks 3, p. 68*

3. Service as a Spiritual Discipline

When we call to mind various spiritual disciplines, or sadhanas, service is usually not the first one we think of. We commonly cite meditation, devotional singing, or study of holy books. Yet service is a potent and complete sadhana. Selfless service is a path to God-realization.

When service is performed from compassion, without desire for reward or recognition, it can be a source of unlimited joy. That joy is found in the happiness of another, in the recognition that we are all manifestations of God. When we practice that discipline, we come to see that God is everywhere. The world is the body of God. All beings and all objects are manifestations of his will. When we find the Lord everywhere, we know that we too are God.

> *You should believe that service is a path to God-realization. Service activities are to be undertaken not for the sake of the Sathya Sai Organization nor for the sake of society. They are purely and essentially for your own sake -- to transform your own lives and redeem yourselves.*
>
> *Sanathana Sarathi, Sept. 84, p. 232*

With time and practice, service becomes an indispensable part of spiritual life. Through service, we learn to see God in all people and all things. Whatever our creed, service opens our hearts and lets the divinity emerge. We can forget our own needs and open up to the needs of others. How better can we serve God than to alleviate the suffering of his children -- and to protect the well-being of Earth and all its creatures?

Service to man will help your divinity to blossom, for it will gladden your heart and make you feel that life has been worthwhile. Service to man is service to God, for God is in every man and every living being and in every stone and stump.

Sathya Sai Speaks 4, p. 178

Service is an excellent arena for the reduction of ego. In service, we must consider the needs of others. We must learn to accept criticism and to persevere despite all obstacles. This spiritual proving ground enables us to see if we have been successful in reducing our anger, impatience, and greed. It allows us to gauge the depths of our compassion and understanding. Spirituality should not exist only in our minds: spiritual principles must be practiced and made strong by the courage of our convictions and self-sacrifice. This type of service reforms us into images of divinity.

But do not believe that you can by means of seva (service) reform or reshape the world. You may or you may not. That does not matter. The real value of seva, its most visible result, is that it reforms you, reshapes you. Do seva as sadhana; then you will be humble and happy.

Sathya Sai Speaks 5, p. 327

The task of eliminating the self-serving ego is not quick or easy. But through service, we learn to negate the pull of the senses toward the objects of wrong desire. Attachment to material pleasures inflates the ego and makes it difficult for us to experience the atma. As a cure to this tendency, service is ideal. It reduces attachment and keeps us mindful of the needs of others and all the kingdoms of nature.

Seva is the best sadhana for eliminating the nefarious pull of the mind towards desire.

Sathya Sai Speaks 7, p. 272

Eliminating the mind's pull toward desire is a major aspect of spiritual endeavor. The benefit of service is that it directs us away from too much self-concern. It is one of the few practices which allows us to escape from the cycle of concentrating on our own needs. When we work for the benefit of others, the Lord looks after our needs.

Selfless service is a more exalted means of spiritual progress than such other ways as meditation, bhajan, and yoga. This is so because when we undertake meditation, japa (repetition of the name of God), or yoga, we do so for our own benefit and not for the good of others. These are aimed at subjugating one's individual desires and securing happiness for oneself. What we should aspire for is the attainment of the good of others without any desire for personal gain.

Summer Showers 1979, pp. 5-6

4. Motivation for Service

God will not ask you, "When and where did you do service?" He will ask, "With what motive did you do it? What was the intention that prompted you?" You may weigh the seva and boast of its quantity. But God seeks quality, the quality of the heart, the purity of the mind, the holiness of the motive.

Sathya Sai Speaks 11, p. 195

Love is the best motivation for service. Love for others and love for God inspire us to true service. Through selfless work for others, we broaden our love and direct it to the God in others. There is no way to serve God except to serve his creation. For what can we give to God? We can offer only our love, intelligence, and labor to those in need.

It (service) is the very essence of bhakti (devotion to God), the very breath of a bhakta (devotee), his very nature. It springs from the actual experience of the bhakta -- an experience that convinces him that all beings are God's children, that all bodies are altars where God is installed, that all places are his residences.

Sathya Sai Speaks 5, p. 237

We endlessly pray to the Lord for his grace. But how can we expect to receive grace if we will not lift our hands to help others? We earn God's love by our selfless actions. To progress on the spiritual path, it is more important for God to love us than for us to love God. We earn his love and grace through selfless service. Sai Baba sets an example of endless giving, never expecting anything in return. We must graduate from spiritual grade school and follow the example. How better can we repay our debt for the blessings we receive than by giving in turn to others? The stream only remains fresh when it gives away the water that it receives.

> *The Lord is pleased only when you do things the Lord desires! How else can you win his grace? How else than by nursing and nourishing, succoring and saving his children?*
> *Sathya Sai Speaks 7, p. 196*

When we start, it is difficult for us to know how to serve. We must carefully appraise our abilities and choose an appropriate field of service. We must learn to be selfless and caring, but just as important, we must be effective and truly helpful. Our service should match our skills and training.

> *You must have not merely enthusiasm to serve, but the intelligence and the skill; then only can you be efficient and useful. Enthusiasm without efficiency is often a source of loss and grief.*
> *Sathya Sai Speaks 5, p. 125*

The quantity of work done is not important. What is important is that service is motivated by pure ideals. We should serve others as we would serve God himself. The one who serves must act without selfishness, anger, or greed. The servant must act without desire of reward or recognition.

> *When judging the service done by a member...it is not the quantity or the number of individual instances that matter; they do not count at all. Judge rather the motive that led him to serve, the genuineness of the love and compassion with which the seva was saturated. The explanation that appeals to Swami is that you did the seva with no taint of ego, and that you derived unsurpassed ananda (joy) as a result.*
> *Sathya Sai Speaks 10, p. 220*

There are many tests for practitioners of service. As in the other spiritual disciplines, the Lord tests us to see that our selflessness is strong and genuine. We must learn to serve despite criticism and obstacles. Our wills must be strong enough to overcome ego and inertia. Obstacles appear to test and strengthen our resolve.

The Lord, too, will provide many tests to ensure that your faith is firm, that your spirit of seva is full and universal. The weaker practitioners of this seva sadhana will soon be shaken by these tests and stray away from the right path.
Sathya Sai Speaks 10, p. 219

5. Crossing the Ocean

During the daytime, a window opens our vision to the horizons. At night, it reflects back only a picture of ourselves. The mind is like a window. It has no color or quality of its own, yet it reflects all that we see. If the light of our intellect is focused outside, it reveals the whole world. If it shines only on ourselves, it reflects a narrow vision of our ego. The act of service helps us to focus outside ourselves. It shows us that we are an inseparable part of the divine creation.

The joy of service grows and blossoms into detachment. When we serve God in others, we find that the Lord is resident in our own hearts also. Desire for personal gain vanishes and we experience lasting happiness. If the essential step of service is not practiced, then how can we know the joy?

One cannot cross the ocean of this cycle of births and deaths by visiting many sacred places, nor can one do it by performing japa and studying sastras (holy books). It is only possible to do so by performing seva, or service.
Summer Showers 1973, p. 75

The spiritual fact is that we can grow only by expressing love in action. The inspiring truth is that we should be grateful to those who allow us to serve them -- who have given us an opportunity to approach closer to God. And most humbling and most exalting -- because all exists in Oneness -- is the fact that when we serve others, we are actually only serving ourselves!

Questions for Study Circle

1. What is service?

2. Why should we serve?

3. What kind of service should we do?

4. Whom do we serve?

5. How does service help us to find God?

6. Is it possible to serve God in other people?

7. How can service reduce our negative qualities?

8. Can we love God and not serve others?

9. Does service please God?

10. Is self-realization possible without doing service for others?

References for Further Study

1. Gita Vahini, pp. 242-243 (Sathwic, rajasic, thamasic charity).

2. Jnana Vahini, p. 36 (Service is not fruitful apart from spiritual practice).

3. Sathya Sai Speaks 5, p. 208 (One cannot serve when the senses drag him away).

4. Sathya Sai Speaks 5, pp. 327-332.

5. Sathya Sai Speaks 6, pp. 79-82, 272-278.

6. Sathya Sai Speaks 8, pp. 1-4.

7. Sathya Sai Speaks 9, pp. 130-133 (Service brings many benefits, including grace).

8. Sathya Sai Speaks 10, p. 54 (Service is the most effective means to reduce ego and realize brotherhood).

9. Sathya Sai Speaks 10, p. 94 (You do service for your own benefit).

10. Sathya Sai Speaks 10, pp. 97-99.

11. Sathya Sai Speaks 11, p. 113 (Service is worship offered to the Lord).

12. Sathya Sai Speaks 11, pp. 198-200.

13. Summer Showers 1973, pp. 75-85.

14. Summer Showers 1974, p. 216 (One should not incur debt to do service).

15. Summer Showers 1979, p. 9 (Merit acquired from service cannot be gained even from rigorous austerity).

APPENDIX

The following sources were used in the preparation of this material. The edition and length in pages are listed to help the reader find the quotations used. Some editions may be longer or shorter in pages, so the length of the source edition should help the reader's research efforts. It is often valuable for the reader to keep in mind the date and context of a reference.

A. The Vahini Series of writings by Sri Sathya Sai Baba first appeared as serialized articles in the monthly magazine *Sanathana Sarathi,* published by the Sri Sathya Sai Baba Books and Publications Trust in Prasanthi Nilayam, India. The Vahinis were first printed in book form by the Sri Sathya Sai Books and Publications Trust. American editions are published by authority granted to the Sathya Sai Baba Society and the Sathya Sai Book Center of America. Grateful acknowledgement is made to these sources.

Dharma Vahini, Fourth Edition 1975. (89 pages)

Dhyana Vahini, American Edition. (76 pages)

Gita Vahini, Fourth Edition 1978. (304 pages)

Jnana Vahini, American Edition. (67 pages)

Prasanthi Vahini, Fourth Edition. (76 pages)

Prema Vahini, American Edition. (97 pages)

Upanishad Vahini, American Edition 1970. (78 pages)

Vidya Vahini, American Edition 1985. (91 pages)

B. Books from the Sathya Sai Speaks series were compiled from discourses by Sri Sathya Sai Baba from 1953 to 1982. They were compiled and edited by N. Kasturi, M.A., B.L., the editor of *Sanathana Sarathi*. These volumes were published by the Sri Sathya Sai Publication and Education Foundation in Prasanthi Nilayam, India. American editions are printed by permission granted to the Sathya Sai Baba Society and Sathya Sai Book Center Of America. Volume Seven is authorized by the Sri Sathya Sai Education Foundation of Bombay.

Sathya Sai Speaks 1, Second American Printing 1984. (196 pages)

Sathya Sai Speaks 2, American Edition. (254 pages)

Sathya Sai Speaks 3, Second American Edition 1970. (235 pages)

Sathya Sai Speaks 4, American Edition. (392 pages)

Sathya Sai Speaks 5, American Edition. (344 pages)

Sathya Sai Speaks 6, American Edition. (336 pages)

Sathya Sai Speaks 7, American Edition. (507 pages)

Sathya Sai Speaks 8, American Edition. (225 pages)

Sathya Sai Speaks 9, American Edition. (234 pages)

Sathya Sai Speaks 10, Second Edition 1981. (316 pages)

Sathya Sai Speaks 11, First American Printing 1986. (306 pages)

C. The Summer Showers volumes were compiled from discourses given by Sri Sathya Sai Baba during the summer courses on Indian Culture and Spirituality at Whitefield, India, from 1972 to 1979. The 1976 series is titled differently, as *Summer Roses on the Blue Mountains*. The 1976 summer course was held at the hill station of Ootacamund in that year. The 1972, 1976, 1977, and 1978 series are published by the Sri Sathya Sai Education and Publication Foundation. The 1973 series in published by the Sri Sathya Sai Education Foundation of Bombay. The Bhagavan Sri Sathya Sai Seva Samithi of New Delhi published the 1974 edition, while the 1979 series was published by the Sri Sathya Sai Hostel at Brindavan, Kadugodi, India. Grateful acknowledgement is made to these sources.

Summer Showers in Brindavan 1972, American Edition. (310 pages)
Summer Showers in Brindavan 1973, American Edition. (274 pages)
Summer Showers in Brindavan 1974, American Edition. (296 pages)
Summer Roses on the Blue Mountains 1977, First Edition. (119 pages)
Summer Showers in Brindavan 1977, First Edition. (254 pages)
Summer Showers in Brindavan 1978, First Edition. (222 pages)
Summer Showers in Brindavan 1979, First Edition. (175 pages)

D. The following two books by Dr. John Hislop, the former President of the Sathya Sai Baba Council of America, have also been quoted. These books are published by Birth Day Publishing Company of San Diego, California. *Conversations With Sathya Sai Baba* was released in 1978 by the Sri Sathya Sai Baba Society of America. *My Baba and I* was released in 1985 by the Sri Sathya Sai Books and Publications Trust.

Conversations With Sathya Sai Baba, 1978. (152 pages)

My Baba And I, 1985, First Edition . (282 pages)

E. Other volumes quoted in *Pathways To God* include the following:

The Rama Story (Ram Katha Rasavahini), Vraj Brindavan Press, Kadugodi, India. By permission of Sri Sathya Sai Education and Publication Foundation. First Edition 1977. (507 pages)

Sai Baba Avatar, Howard Murphet. Birth Day Publishing Co. 1977, San Diego, California. (222 pages)

Sanathana Sarathi, the monthly magazine distributed by the Sri Sathya Sai Books and Publications Trust in Prasanthi Nilayam, India.

Sandeha Nivarini, States People Press, Bombay. Fifth Edition 1970. By permission of Sri Sathya Sai Education Foundation. (141 pages)

Teachings of Sri Sathya Sai Baba, CSA Press, Lakemont Georgia. By permission of Sri Sathya Sai Book Center, Tustin, California.1974 Edition. (144 pages)